T0284491

MIND MELD

www.royalcollins.com

MIND MELD

THE RISE OF THE
BRAIN-COMPUTER
INTERFACE

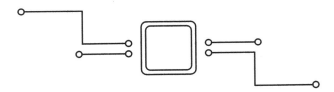

KEVIN CHEN

Books Beyond Boundaries

ROYAL COLLINS

Mind Meld: The Rise of the Brain-Computer Interface

Kevin Chen

First published in 2024 by Royal Collins Publishing Group Inc.
Groupe Publication Royal Collins Inc.
550-555 boul. René-Lévesque O Montréal (Québec) H2Z1B1 Canada

10 9 8 7 6 5 4 3 2 1

ISBN: 978-1-4878-1180-8

To find out more about our publications, please visit www.royalcollins.com.

CONTENTS

CONTENTS

PREFACE

In the quest to understand the brain's mysteries, we often find ourselves at the crossroads of legend and science, myth and reality. The questions that beckon us are as profound as they are perplexing:

1. What becomes of us when the brain, our command center, is compromised or lost?
2. Can the fusion of brain and computer herald a revolution in human capabilities?
3. Is it conceivable for human consciousness to achieve immortality through digital networking?

These questions, emerging from the depths of our quest for knowledge, are gradually being answered as we journey through the uncharted realms of brain science.

Our story begins with a legend from China's ancient book from the Han Dynasty, *The Classic of Mountains and Seas*. It speaks of Xingtian, a minister of Emperor Yan, known for his defiance against the Yellow Emperor. In a fierce battle, Xingtian was beheaded, but rather than succumbing to death, he stood up, defiant as ever. With his chest's nipples transformed into eyes and his navel into a mouth, he continued his eternal struggle against the heavens. Though steeped in myth, this ancient narrative reflects the profound human pondering over life, death, and the enigma of the brain. It portrays a belief that the loss of the physical brain does not necessarily equate to the end of existence—a testament to the ancient understanding of the brain as a vessel of the life force *qi*.

Fast forward to over 1,700 years ago, during the Three Kingdoms era in China. The famed statesman Cao Cao, plagued by debilitating headaches, sought the expertise of the legendary physician Hua Tuo. Hua Tuo's radical proposition of a craniotomy to alleviate Cao Cao's suffering was met with suspicion and fear, culminating in the tragic demise of both men. This historical account from the *Romance of the Three Kingdoms* signifies a pivotal moment in the evolving Chinese perception of the brain—a shift from seeing it as merely an organ to acknowledging its critical role in health and well-being.

These tales from antiquity, both mythological and historical, mirror a global journey of discovery about the brain. They mark the progression from early beliefs shrouded in mysticism to a more nuanced understanding grounded in medical science.

Now, let us leap into the future—the year 2035 in Shanghai, where the line between science fiction and reality is increasingly blurred. Dr. Li Ming prepares to embark on a groundbreaking procedure in a room where technology and human resilience converge. His patient, Yang Jia, embodies the hope and potential of this new era. Despite the darkness cast by her genetic condition, she sits ready for a test that could redefine the limits of human perception.

In this carefully orchestrated setting, a brain-computer interface (BCI) device, no larger than a button, is poised to unlock a new world for Yang Jia. This device, glowing softly with the promise of technological marvel, represents the culmination of years of research and the dawn of a new chapter in medical science.

This scene, reminiscent of a futuristic novel, is a figment of imagination and a glimpse into the imminent reality. As visionaries like Elon Musk push the boundaries of BCI technology, we find ourselves on the cusp of a new era—one where the integration of brain and machine could redefine our very existence.

In this book, we delve deep into the world of BCIs. We explore their evolution from nascent concepts to sophisticated tools poised to transform healthcare, education, and entertainment. We unravel the stories of medical breakthroughs on the horizon, where restored senses and reclaimed lives are no longer just hopeful aspirations but imminent realities. We examine the transformative role of BCIs in education and gaming, where barriers are shattered, and new realms of experience are unlocked.

But our journey through this book is more than merely exploring technological advancements. It reflects on the essence of human identity in an age where the lines between consciousness and digital intelligence blur. As we venture through these pages, we invite you to contemplate the ethical landscape surrounding BCIs to envision a world where human cognition and digital intelligence are inextricably linked.

Welcome to the transformative era of BCI—an epoch where science fiction merges with reality, where the capabilities of the human brain are expanded beyond imagination, and where the language of neurons and bytes is shaping the future of humanity.

As you turn these pages, you are not just reading about a technological revolution; you are stepping into a realm where the mysteries of the brain unfold, promising a future as intriguing as the legends of old.

CHAPTER 1

ENTERING THE BRAIN-COMPUTER ERA

1.1 *The Matrix*: From Science Fiction to Reality

Over twenty years ago, *The Matrix* emerged as a groundbreaking science fiction film. Today, its status as a cinematic icon remains unchallenged. *The Matrix* weaves an allegory of human and machine civilizations, crafting an expansive cyberpunk universe.

In this world, humans are subjugated by machines, unknowingly trapped in a simulated reality while their bioenergy is harvested. It's only with the arrival of Neo, the protagonist, that the illusion is shattered. Using BCI technology, Neo battles against the mechanical overlords, challenging the boundaries of virtual and actual realities.

The Matrix was visionary, intertwining concepts of free will, artificial intelligence (AI), and BCIs. The film envisaged a world where knowledge could be directly downloaded into the brain, bypassing conventional learning methods. This portrayal of BCIs, where a simple connection to the brain could alter perceived reality, was imaginative and prophetic.

The fascination with BCIs isn't limited to *The Matrix*. Other science fiction narratives, like *Attack on Titan* and *Alita: Battle Angel*, explore protagonists enhanced by BCIs, engaging in high-stakes battles. William Gibson's *Winter*

Market features a character who, despite a congenital disability, achieves a form of immortality by transferring consciousness into a computer program, thanks to BCI.

These once-fanciful ideas are inching closer to reality. The 21st century is witnessing the dawn of an era where science fiction scenarios are materializing, driven by cutting-edge technologies. BCIs, arguably the most sci-fi of these technologies, raise significant ethical debates about the interplay between humanity and technology, a topic I will delve into in the final chapter of this book.

One notable figure who leveraged BCI technology was the renowned physicist Stephen Hawking. Despite severe physical paralysis, Hawking communicated with the world through a BCI enabled wheelchair, transforming his thoughts into text.

BCIs are currently gaining traction, particularly for their potential in medicine. The 2019 Tribeca Film Festival featured the documentary *I Am Human*, spotlighting this technology. The film follows three patients, each hoping to regain lost abilities through BCI therapy: Bill, paralyzed from a biking accident; Steven, blinded by a congenital condition; and Annie, slowed by Parkinson's disease.

The documentary details their transformative journeys. Bill regains some motor control, Steven perceives shapes and colors, and Annie improves her mobility and expression. These cases highlight the profound impact of BCIs, offering a glimpse into a future where the lines between human cognition and machine assistance blur.

As *I Am Human* director Taryn Southern remarked, the reality of brain technology today rivals the visions of science fiction. With thousands already benefiting from BCI implants and millions more anticipated by 2029, the era of the brain-computer interface is not just a distant dream but an unfolding reality.

The Matrix, once a bold cinematic vision, is morphing into our present, marking the advent of the brain-computer age. A world where the fantastical becomes feasible, and the lines between human and machine grow ever more indistinct.

1.2 Deciphering Brain-Computer Interfaces

1.2.1 From Verbal Communication to Brain-Computer Interfaces

Language, a hallmark of human cognition, has been eloquently described by David Purpel, a professor of psychology and neuroscience at New York University. In his paper in *Science Advances*, he likens language to a mechanism where sound waves compress information into our minds.

The journey from hearing speech to comprehending it is a complex neural process. Initially, the auditory cortex translates sound waves into neural signals. Neurophysiological studies reveal that brain waves within this cortex fluctuate in frequency, corresponding to the intensity of these sound waves. These fluctuations, akin to a surfer riding the undulations of the ocean, help the brain segment auditory signals. This segmentation is crucial for syllable differentiation and semantic recognition, breaking down lengthy linguistic streams into manageable informational chunks.

The emergence of human language was not an overnight phenomenon but a product of extensive evolution. Tracing back, we see a progression from simple neuropeptides and neurons to intricate neural networks, from primitive ganglia to the sophisticated neocortex. This developmental journey epitomizes a leap from basic survival instincts, governed by the reptilian brain, to complex emotional processing in the limbic system and ultimately to rational thought and abstraction in the neocortex.

About 100,000 years ago, humankind achieved a monumental breakthrough: associating specific sounds with specific objects. For instance, the word "stone" isn't the object itself but a symbolic representation. This abstraction marked the genesis of primitive language. By 50000 BC, humans could communicate with fully formed languages, converting intricate thoughts into sound symbols capable of traversing through air vibrations to other minds, making them comprehensible.

The advent of language labeled the world symbolically and enabled humans to learn vicariously. This ability to absorb indirect experiences significantly bolstered human survival. The language was a conduit for wisdom to flow across generations, amassing into a tribal knowledge base. As this collective wisdom grew, so did productivity and labor efficiency, propelling humanity into urbanization and, eventually, the industrial revolution.

In the present era of rapid information technology development and AI breakthroughs, human learning capacity seems dwarfed by AI. Ironically, once a cornerstone of human advancement, language reveals its inherent flaws: low precision and efficiency. The social and ambiguous nature of human language often leads to communication inaccuracies. Furthermore, the speed at which we input and process language-based information pales compared to digital technologies.

As we enter the digital era, these human limitations become increasingly apparent. History's relentless march drives technological innovation, setting the stage for the revolutionary advent of the BCI. BCIs promise to transcend the barriers of traditional language, offering a direct, efficient conduit between human thought and digital communication.

1.2.2 What Is a BCI?

A BCI is a revolutionary system that bridges the brain and a computer, creating a direct communication pathway. This interface facilitates a two-way transfer of information: from the brain to the computer, enabling control over external devices, and from the computer back to the brain, where it can stimulate neural activity through electrical signals.

To break it down, a BCI consists of three essential components: the brain, machine, and interface. In this context, the brain refers to the physical brain or nervous system, extending beyond just the abstract concept of the mind. The machine component encompasses any computational or processing device—ranging from basic circuits to sophisticated silicon chips and extending to various external apparatuses. The interface is the intermediary for exchanging information, thus forming the crucial link in the BCI equation: Brain + Machine + Interface.

A BCI is a machine's method to directly read and interpret brain signals, enabling interaction with external devices without relying on the traditional output pathways of peripheral nerves and muscles. This system captures parameters like electrical fields, magnetic fields, or hemoglobin oxygenation produced by brain activity. These signals are then relayed to a computer for processing and interpretation.

The implications of BCIs are profound. They represent a new paradigm in information communication and interaction, surpassing traditional verbal communication in precision and efficiency. BCIs have the unique capability to capture and record fleeting thoughts with unparalleled accuracy. Moreover, they hold immense potential in medical applications, offering new avenues for treating neurological conditions and restoring functions impaired by brain-related issues. In essence, BCIs are not just an interface but a gateway to a new era of human-machine interaction.

1.3 A Century of BCI Evolution

While BCIs have surged to the forefront of scientific and technological research only recently, their story stretches back much further, revealing a rich and intricate history. BCIs, renowned for bypassing the usual efferent pathways of peripheral nerves and muscles, capture and analyze the brain's bioelectrical signals. This groundbreaking approach has established a direct communication and control pathway between the brain and electronic devices like computers.

This evolution of BCIs is deeply intertwined with the advancements in brain science and the burgeoning field of microelectronics. As we delve into this journey, we uncover a fascinating tapestry of interdisciplinary progress and innovation. BCIs are not just a recent phenomenon but a culmination of a century's exploration and discovery in understanding the brain's complex mechanisms and integrating these insights with cutting-edge technology.

1.3.1 Phase 1: Theoretical Understanding of Brain Structure

The journey of BCIs begins with a foundational moment in the history of neuroscience. In 1924, Hans Berger, a German psychiatrist often hailed as the father of the electroencephalogram, recorded the first electrical signals from the human brain. He coined this groundbreaking phenomenon as

"Electroencephalogram," or EEG. His seminal work was published in 1929 in the *Archives of Psychiatry*, establishing the EEG's significance in brain research.

It was in 1938 that American neurologist Herbert Jasper envisioned the potential of decoding language from brainwaves in a Christmas card to Berger. This concept, which now seems like an early sci-fi depiction of BCIs, marked the beginning of academic exploration into technologies related to BCIs.

This era was pivotal in deepening our theoretical understanding of brain structure. The role of EEG neurofeedback mechanisms has become particularly significant for today's development of BCIs. The brain, humanity's most unique organ, comprises hundreds of billions of neurons and is divided into key areas: the cerebrum (the center of thought), the cerebellum (coordinating movement), and the brainstem (the primitive yet vital connector for the cerebrum, cerebellum, and spinal cord).

The brainstem, while primitive, regulates critical life functions like respiration, body temperature, and swallowing. It's also home to the "reticular activating system," essential for maintaining consciousness. Damage to the brainstem can be instantaneously fatal, highlighting its crucial role in human survival.

Regarding brain structure, the complexity escalates. The brain, as the hub of the nervous system and conductor of bodily functions, has areas corresponding to specific cognitive functions like vision, touch, hearing, language, and movement. These areas generate the electrical signals vital for BCI operation.

Focusing on the brain's role in the central nervous system, which houses about 87 billion neurons, it continually receives and processes signals from various nerves, including optic and auditory. The brain analyzes these inputs, generating responses to the external environment through motor signals, which then control our actions via the Peripheral Nervous System (PNS).

When neurons transmit signals, they create detectable electromagnetic signals. When many neurons work in concert, these signals can be picked up by macroscopic electrodes, allowing researchers to analyze brain activity. Initially, scientists studied EEG waveforms in the time domain, later employing Fourier or wavelet transformations for frequency domain analysis. Considering the brain's inherent complexity and non-linearity, introducing chaos dynamics led to applying tools like fractal dimension (FD) in analyzing brainwaves.

This phase laid the groundwork for the intricate field of BCIs, bridging the gap between theoretical neuroscience and practical technological application.

1.3.2 Phase 2: Decoding Brain Signal Applications

The journey of BCIs took a significant leap thirty years after the discovery of brain waves. In 1969, German professor Eberhard Erich Fetz pioneered an experiment with monkeys that laid the groundwork for early BCI applications. Using operant conditioning, Fetz enabled monkeys to control a dashboard pointer through specific thought patterns. This experiment demonstrated that the activity of a single neuron in the primate's motor cortex could be harnessed to control an external device, marking a nascent form of BCI before the term was even coined.

Fetz's groundbreaking study connected a monkey's neuron to a dashboard. The monkey could trigger the neuron by focusing its thoughts in a certain way, causing the dashboard to rotate and earning a food reward. This experiment showed that the monkey learned to control the dashboard through brain activity alone, a remarkable feat for the time.

This early success spurred further research in decoding brain signals for practical applications. By 1970, the US Defense Advanced Research Projects Agency (DARPA) had initiated a program exploring brain communication via EEG. Then, in 1973, UCLA professor Jacques Vidal published a seminal paper, "On Direct Brain-Computer Communication," where he formally introduced the concept and definition of a "brain-computer interface." Vidal's work emphasized the potential of BCIs in neural repair, aiming to assist patients in restoring lost senses and motor functions. His contributions officially established BCI as an independent field of research.

Technological progress soon led to the first neuroprosthetic devices for humans in the mid-1990s. A significant milestone was achieved in 1998 when Emory University researcher Philip Kennedy implanted a BCI device into a human. This procedure connected the human brain to a computer, remotely enabling cursor control. Termed "Brain Gate," this technology represented a major advancement in BCI research.

BCIs were garnering increasing attention; their ability to facilitate brain-computer communication without the need for peripheral nerves and muscles highlighted their potential in treating disabling conditions like stroke and epilepsy. This phase of BCI development underscored the technology's profound impact on medicine and neuroscience, paving the way for future innovations.

1.3.3 Phase 3: From Laboratory to Marketplace

As we ventured into the 21st century, the focus on BCIs shifted significantly toward practical applications. This era saw BCIs transitioning from purely academic research to tangible market-ready technologies, driven by the contributions of an increasing number of dedicated researchers.

A pivotal figure in this phase was Miguel Nicolelis, often called the "Father of BCIs." His groundbreaking work under John Chapin at Hahnemann University in the 1990s significantly advanced our understanding of brain function. During this time, two predominant theories in brain neuroscience were debated: the "distributed network theory," suggesting that neurons form continuous networks, and the "localization theory," positing that neurons operate independently. Nicolelis and Chapin, proponents of the former, developed innovative methods to study how many neurons collaborate in animal behavior.

To validate their hypothesis, Nicolelis leveraged BCI technology. In a landmark 2000 study at Duke University, he demonstrated how EEG signals from a monkey's cerebral cortex could control a robot thousands of miles away in real-time—a feat aptly described as "Monkey Think, Robot Do." This study advanced our understanding of neural network learning mechanisms and marked a significant step toward developing controllable prosthetics.

Fourteen years later, Nicolelis introduced the world to the first brain-controlled exoskeleton, "Bra-Santos Dumont." This device allowed the brain to control exoskeleton activity while relaying sensory feedback like touch, temperature, and force back to the wearer. The technology made a sensational debut with paraplegic teenager Giuliano Pinto at Brazil's 2014 FIFA World Cup opening ceremony. Pinto, who had been paralyzed from the chest down due to a car accident, used a BCI to transmit signals from his brain, bypassing his spinal injury, to control a wearable mech. This enabled him to perform the symbolic kickoff, an event described by a TV commentator as "a small step for Pinto, but a giant leap for BCI technology."

Pinto's journey, which involved ten months of training through the Walk Again Program initiated by Nicolelis, significantly improved his spinal injury rating. His progress demonstrated that basic science could lead to extraordinary, unanticipated breakthroughs when applied innovatively.

Nicolelis's reflections on these achievements underscore the transformative potential of BCIs: "It goes to show that sometimes basic science can lead you to places you never imagined and bring about unexpected discoveries."

1.3.4 Phase 4: The Technology Explosion

As we moved through the early stages of understanding brain structure, decoding brain signals, and transitioning from lab to market, BCIs have finally stepped into the limelight of commercialization. Since 2000, when Duke University's Professor Miguel Nicolelis demonstrated the feasibility of controllable prosthetics, BCIs have entered an era of technological explosion, brought myriad breakthroughs, and edged closer to market readiness.

In 2004, Cyberkinetics, a US company, received Food and Drug Administration (FDA) approval and launched clinical trials for a motor cortex BCI. In these trials, Matthew Nagle, a 25-year-old man paralyzed for four years, became the first patient to receive a long-term BCI implant. Post-implant, he managed tasks like email, drawing, and controlling a TV remote through thought alone, using robotic limbs. The device, BrainGate, contained 96 electrodes (Utah Array) in the motor cortex, corresponding to the arm and hand. This technology showcased the potential of BCIs in restoring motor functions in disabled patients.

Fast forward to September 2016, researchers at Stanford University implanted BCIs in two monkeys. One monkey astoundingly typed Shakespeare's "To be or not to be, that is the question" in just one minute. In October, Nathan Copeland, a volunteer, controlled a robotic arm and experienced a groundbreaking "handshake" with US President Barack Obama. This handshake was unique— Copeland controlled the robotic arm and "felt" the touch, thanks to sensors in the arm's fingers linked to electrodes in his sensory cortex.

In December, Professor Bin He and his team at the University of Minnesota managed object control in three-dimensional space using scalp EEGs without brain implants. This research is expected to aid millions with disabilities and neurological disorders.

In April 2019, University of California-San Francisco neurosurgeon Edward Chang implanted a high-density electrode array into a quadriplegic patient, decoding words and sentences from cortical activity in real-time. This breakthrough in speech synthesis from brain activity has profound implications for communication in speech-impaired individuals.

Meanwhile, Elon Musk's Neuralink announced a major advancement in BCI technology. Using a neurosurgical robot, Neuralink's system implants 96 ultra-fine "wires" with 3,072 electrode sites in the brain, all read through a USB-C interface. This system presents less brain damage, more channels, and an aesthetically pleasing design.

In China, a team from Zhejiang University and its Second Affiliated Hospital completed the nation's first clinical research on implantable BCIs. An elderly paralyzed patient, after surgery and training, could control a robotic arm for eating and drinking.

By the end of 2020, Shanghai Ruijin Hospital began research involving 26 patients, with results in 2023 showing significant improvements in depressive symptoms using BCI technology. The trial, named "BCI Neuromodulation Treatment of Refractory Depression Clinical Trial," involved implanting a "brain pacemaker" and two electrodes in the brain. Patients could instantly uplift their mood by turning on an "external switch."

In June 2023, China announced a breakthrough in BCI for the Chinese language. Researchers from Fudan University, Shanghai University of Science and Technology, and Tianjin University developed a modular, multiplexed parallel neural network method to synthesize Chinese speech from implantable neural recordings. This represents the first use of ECoG for Chinese syllable decoding and speech synthesis, offering potential solutions for patients with tonal language speech impairments.

The advancements in BCIs extend beyond these milestones, with rapid development occurring in unexplored areas. Dr. Miguel A. Nicolelis and Dr. Ronald M. Cicurel's book, *The Relativistic Brain*, reflects on this progress, drawing an analogy to Caesar crossing the Rubicon River. Just as Caesar's crossing marked the start of a new epoch, so has our exploration of BCIs. Standing on the other side of the metaphorical Rubicon, BCI technology is soaring, becoming one of the most groundbreaking and disruptive technologies of the 21st century.

1.4 Three Ways to Connect with the Brain

BCI technology operates through a process that includes signal collection, signal processing and command output, execution by end devices, and feedback. Each stage utilizes distinct technologies to transfer information to the next phase. Signal collection, the initial stage of BCIs, can be categorized into three types: invasive, non-invasive, and interventional.

1.4.1 Invasive Brain-Computer Interfaces

Invasive BCIs collect electrophysiological signals generated by brain tissue. This requires directly inserting electrodes into the brain tissue or attaching them to the brain's surface. These electrodes detect electrical activity from either individual neurons or neural networks in their vicinity, allowing for real-time and accurate monitoring of local neural network dynamics.

The most crucial component in invasive BCIs is the implantable electrode, an electrical element in direct contact with brain tissue. The most commonly used implantable electrodes are of two types:

1. Microelectrode Arrays. The Utah Electrode Array (UEA) from Blackrock Neurotech is a prominent example. It consists of hundreds of needle-like electrodes forming a multi-channel array, implanted 1–3 mm deep into the brain cortex. Each electrode, about 80 μm in diameter, records neural signals within a 0.5 mm radius of its tip.
2. Electrocorticography (ECoG). These consist of sparse metal contacts forming an array. They are fixed on the surface of the brain cortex, causing less tissue damage than UEA. Each contact covers a larger area and records neural signals within a 1 mm radius and 0.5–3 mm depth, though with less precision than microelectrode arrays and cannot distinguish single-cell signals.

In terms of functionality and transmission efficiency, invasive BCIs offer the best brain-machine communication. They surpass non-invasive types in signal strength, precision, and developmental prospects. However, they also present higher safety risks and costs and require substantial social and ethical considerations. Invasive BCIs necessitate craniotomy, and the electrode insertion process inevitably causes tissue damage, posing high risks to users. The foreign bodies can also trigger immune responses and scar tissue formation, leading to signal degradation or loss.

Once implanted in the brain, electronic components and micropower sources face corrosion risks from prolonged exposure to bodily fluids. This corrosion and the subsequent release of metals and chemicals can impact brain nerves. These safety concerns are critical focus areas for research institutions and regulatory bodies.

1.4.2 Non-invasive BCIs

Non-invasive BCIs represent an external interface approach, requiring no penetration into the brain. Instead, wearable devices are attached to the scalp to record and interpret brain information.

These interfaces typically collect brain signals by fixing electrodes to the scalp's surface, capturing weak electrical signals (Electroencephalograms or EEGs) conducted through the skull from the brain cortex. The advantage of EEGs is their non-invasive nature; metal electrodes are simply placed at specific head locations to gather data. EEG electrodes fall into two categories: wet and dry. Wet electrodes require an electrolytic gel between the electrode and skin to reduce resistance and ensure stable, reliable signals. Dry electrodes, in contrast, directly use conductive materials for skin contact, simplifying the setup but providing less detailed EEG signals. While wet electrodes are preferred in scientific and medical contexts for their superior signal quality, tech companies aiming to bring EEG technology to consumers often opt for dry electrodes for user convenience.

Apart from scalp-collected EEGs, other non-invasive methods used in BCI systems include functional Near-Infrared Spectroscopy (fNIRS), functional Magnetic Resonance Imaging (fMRI), and Magnetoencephalography (MEG).

1. **fNIRS** capitalizes on the scattering properties of blood components under 600–900 nm near-infrared light to detect changes in oxyhemoglobin and deoxyhemoglobin during brain activity. This method is cost-effective, portable, and less noise-resistant but lacks high spatial and temporal resolution.

2. **fMRI** uses magnetic resonance to measure hemodynamic changes triggered by neuronal activity. It offers precise spatial resolution, enabling specific brain region analysis. However, its high cost, large size, and moderate temporal resolution limit its widespread BCI application.

3. **MEG** records magnetic field signals produced by post-synaptic potentials in neurons, indirectly inferring neural electrical activity. MEG offers better spatial resolution than EEG and is less affected by intervening tissues. However, its sensitivity to environmental interference requires specialized shielding, and the equipment is expensive and cumbersome.

It's worth noting that while non-invasive BCIs avoid costly and risky surgeries, the signals they capture are attenuated by the skull and blurred by muscle/skin tissues. This attenuation and dispersion make it challenging to pinpoint the exact brain region or individual neuron responsible for the signals. Consequently, non-invasive BCIs, while safer and simpler to use, still need to catch up to invasive BCIs in effectiveness. Nonetheless, due to a simpler and safer collection process, their broader applicability and audience appeal make non-invasive BCIs a promising development area in various fields.

1.4.3 Interventional Brain-Computer Interfaces

Interventional signal collection for BCIs, a pioneering method, involves implanting electrodes within the brain's vascular inner walls. This minimally invasive technique, known as Endovascular EEG, employs a catheter in the user's neck vessel to position a collapsible stent-like electrode near specific brain cortical areas. Upon expansion, the electrode captures brain electrical signals by adhering to the vessel's inner wall.

The Stentrode, developed by US-based company Synchron, is a significant advancement in this field. Initially designated as a "Breakthrough Medical Device" by the US FDA in 2020, the Stentrode has made remarkable progress. In a 2024 study, six individuals with severe paralysis used the Stentrode in everyday environments, marking a pivotal moment in BCI technology. Unlike traditional invasive BCIs, the Stentrode's implantation does not require craniotomy, significantly reducing associated risks. Its electrodes, which do not directly contact brain tissue, provide signal quality comparable to ECoG electrodes, with stable and effective long-term signal acquisition.

These advancements position interventional BCIs, particularly the Stentrode, at the forefront of brain signal collection technology. They offer a minimally invasive approach, reducing risks associated with conventional brain surgeries. The Stentrode's success in real-world applications, enabling users to perform computer tasks through thought, underscores its potential for FDA review and broader clinical application. This evolution reflects a new direction in BCI exploration, leveraging vascular mediation for safer and more effective brain-computer interaction.

1.5 BCIs: A Timely Technology

As we witness the convergence and continuous exploration of fields like computer science, neurobiology, mathematics, and rehabilitative medicine, BCI technology is transitioning from basic research to market viability. According to a 2020 McKinsey report, the global economic impact of the BCI industry could reach US$70 billion to US$200 billion annually over the next ten to twenty years.

On one hand, fundamental insights into brain mechanisms pave the way for novel treatments for brain diseases. Conversely, BCIs are poised to become the next-generation interactive technology over the next decade, with thought-controlled machines and brain-operated switches becoming a reality. The brain reading and writing interaction technology built on BCIs will bring unprecedented transformations to human society, surpassing even the disruptive nature of AI.

Research by Silicon Valley Live indicates diverse applications of BCI technology across industries. In healthcare, BCIs are used in devices, brain monitoring systems, and treatments for conditions like Attention Deficit Hyperactivity Disorder (ADHD). In education, they assist in memory training and academic coaching. The gaming industry sees BCIs combined with VR/AR for mind-controlled devices and characters. In smart homes, they integrate with Internet of Things (IoT) technologies for thought-controlled appliances.

Looking at healthcare, BCIs facilitate direct interaction between the brain and external devices, bypassing conventional brain information output pathways. With modern medicine's deepening understanding of brain structure and function, BCIs are widely applied in diagnostics, monitoring, and rehabilitation for neurological and psychiatric disorders. The healthcare sector currently represents the largest and fastest-growing market for BCIs.

Outside healthcare, BCIs find potential applications in other non-medical fields. In entertainment, BCIs are merging with toys and VR/AR technologies. Products like brain-controlled cars and VR/AR devices are emerging. Particularly in gaming, BCIs combined with VR allow players to control games through thought, enhancing entertainment and accessibility for players with physical disabilities.

In 2020, the tech company Cognixion released a BCI-based AR headset for immersive experiences across various scenarios, including gaming and telecommunication. Yunrui Intelligent developed the Udrone, a mind-controlled drone.

BCIs are revolutionizing teaching methods and learning processes in education, potentially overhauling existing educational models. For example, BCIs can monitor students' brain states in real-time, establishing personalized teaching environments based on the relationship between brain states and academic performance. A joint team from Tsinghua University's Psychology Department and Education Research Institute has identified neurophysiological markers related to math anxiety, which can be alleviated using BCI and neurofeedback technologies.

In everyday life, especially in smart homes, BCIs enable control of home appliances through the measurement and extraction of central nervous system signals. They form a closed-loop system with external devices, allowing intelligent integration of brain and machine. BCIs act as "remote controls," enabling users to operate lights, doors, curtains, and even smart home robots through thought. Brain-to-brain networking based on BCIs represents an even more advanced and potential area of research and application.

Finally, BCIs are at the forefront of research and experimental application in the military. Soldiers could issue combat commands to weapons through brain signal collectors, enhancing combat capabilities and reducing casualties. The data can be used to analyze and enhance military skills by monitoring soldiers' physiological and psychological states. DARPA's 2015 project Brain-Swarm Interaction and Control Interfaces enables pilots to control aircraft and multiple drones simultaneously through thought.

CHAPTER 2

THE MEDICAL MISSION OF BRAIN-COMPUTER INTERFACES

2.1 Revolutionizing Future Healthcare with Brain-Computer Interfaces

Currently, in a period of exploration and accumulation, BCIs extend beyond entertainment and education, with healthcare being the earliest, most direct, and closest field to commercialization.

In healthcare, BCI applications can be broadly categorized into five scenarios: diagnosis and treatment of limb movement disorders, applications in consciousness and cognitive disorders, applications in mental illness, applications in sensory deficits, and applications in epilepsy and neurodevelopmental disorders.

2.1.1 Diagnosis and Treatment of Limb Movement Disorders

Limb movement disorders, such as amputation or spinal cord injury, not only severely impact physical functions but also profoundly affect patients' psychological well-being and quality of life. Various conditions like cerebral hemorrhage, trauma, stroke, and neurodegenerative diseases like amyotrophic lateral sclerosis (ALS) can lead to impaired limb control. BCIs can significantly improve patients' conditions and quality of life in this domain, offering therapeutic support.

There are mainly two approaches to applying BCIs in treating limb movement disorders:

1. **Assistive BCIs** capture patients' movement intentions to control external devices like prosthetics or exoskeletons. By directly connecting the brain to these devices, BCIs enable the thought-controlled operation of prosthetics and wheelchairs, restoring some lost functions and enhancing patients' independence and quality of life. The process involves four steps: signal collection (using EEG or MEG to capture brain activity), signal processing and decoding (translating brain signals into instructions for external devices), controlling external devices (such as prosthetics to execute the intended movement), and providing feedback (visual or tactile) to help patients achieve more accurate control.

Assistive BCIs enable patients with limb movement disorders to regain mobility and enhance their independence and social interaction. However, challenges remain, such as improving the stability and accuracy of brain signals and requiring systematic training for patients to master BCI operation.

2. **Rehabilitative BCIs** play a vital role in the rehabilitation of limb movement disorders. Due to the plasticity of the central nervous system, repetitive feedback stimulation through BCIs can strengthen neuronal synaptic connections, facilitating repair. This method directly affects the brain's neural plasticity, promoting functional recovery and reconstruction in damaged areas. It works by real-time monitoring of brain activity and sending feedback to the brain, enhancing neuronal connections and synaptic strengthening, thus achieving rehabilitative effects.

The central nervous system's plasticity allows adaptation and repair of damaged neural circuits through appropriate stimulation and training. Rehabilitative BCIs utilize this principle to repetitively stimulate the damaged area, encouraging neurons to reestablish connections. Personalization is crucial in this approach, as each patient's neural plasticity and rehabilitation needs vary.

Rehabilitative BCI technology offers an innovative pathway for patients with limb movement disorders, holding great promise for the future.

2.1.2 Diagnosing and Treating Consciousness and Cognitive Disorders

Consciousness and cognitive disorders, severely impacting cognition functions like awareness, thinking, memory, and emotions, include but are not limited to stroke, brain injury, and neurodegenerative diseases. These conditions can lead to loss of speech, motor abilities, and even awareness of self and surroundings. For example, many patients fall into comas due to traumatic brain injury, stroke, or hypoxic-ischemic encephalopathy, eventually entering a prolonged state of consciousness disorder, such as a vegetative state. However, there is currently no systematic or standardized treatment for such conditions. Accelerating the recovery of consciousness and cognitive functions in these patients has become a pressing clinical challenge.

The advancement of BCI technology offers new possibilities for addressing this clinical dilemma. By capturing and analyzing patients' brain signals through BCIs, clinicians can assess patients' states of consciousness, facilitating diagnosis, prognosis, and even communication with patients with consciousness disorders.

Specifically, BCIs can record EEG signals, reflecting neuronal activities in the brain cortex. Physicians can determine patients' consciousness states by capturing and analyzing these signals. Patients' brain signals may exhibit specific patterns, particularly in coma or vegetative states, providing insights into their consciousness levels.

To further confirm patients' states, physicians can employ targeted stimuli. In this process, auditory, visual, or tactile stimuli are presented to the patient, while unrelated stimuli are shown with higher probability. When patients under BCI monitoring receive targeted stimuli, specific brain responses may occur closely related to their consciousness states. Sometimes, patients exhibit distinct brain responses to certain stimuli, which can indicate potential consciousness recovery.

However, the use of BCIs in this field still needs to be improved. The performance consistency of BCIs can be affected by fluctuations in patients' consciousness and short attention spans. Furthermore, the application of BCIs in this area is still in the research phase, with complex paradigms. Training patients can be time-consuming, and clinicians often find it challenging to master this technology.

2.1.3 Treating Mental Illness with Brain-Computer Interfaces

In recent years, the prevalence of mental illnesses has been on the rise, creating an urgent need for improved mental and psychological health care for many specific populations. Mental illnesses, encompassing various psychological and behavioral disorders, often require long-term treatment and care. Traditional treatment methods, such as pharmacotherapy and psychotherapy, have their limitations. For instance, research indicates that nearly 30% of patients with depression are treatment-resistant, and conventional methods like medication, physical therapy, and cognitive-behavioral therapy show limited effectiveness for these individuals. Therefore, the development of new treatment approaches is essential, and the rapid advancement of BCI technology offers promising prospects for improving research and treatment of challenging mental disorders.

In specific mental illnesses like depression, obsessive-compulsive disorder (OCD), and schizophrenia, BCIs hold the potential for significant impact. Through input-based interfaces, BCI devices can modulate the nervous system, promoting positive changes in abnormal brain structures and functions, thus aiding in rehabilitating neuropsychiatric diseases.

Specifically, brain electrical signals provide richer and deeper emotional information than other physiological signals. BCI devices, employing learning algorithms, can extract features from EEG signals to recognize and analyze various emotions. This technology can aid in understanding the mechanisms of neuropsychiatric diseases like depression and anxiety and also serve as a tool in adjunctive treatment.

Neurofeedback training with BCI devices also shows potential in the rehabilitative treatment of mental illnesses. Patients can gradually regulate their emotions and cognition by enabling them to observe their own EEG signals and understand the link between their emotional states and brain activity. This neurofeedback training can positively contribute to the rehabilitation of conditions like depression and anxiety, helping patients establish healthier emotional regulation mechanisms.

Of course, BCI technology is still in an ongoing development and exploration phase. While it shows immense potential in the realm of mental illnesses, there are challenges in practical application. Issues like the stability and accuracy of the technology, along with privacy concerns, need further resolution. Additionally, the diagnosis and treatment of mental illnesses require a comprehensive consideration of various factors, with BCI technology being one of the potential methods.

2.1.4 Diagnosing and Treating Sensory Deficits

Humans possess various sensory organs, like those for hearing, vision, and touch, which, after initial processing, relay information to corresponding functional areas of the brain cortex. Modern medicine has elucidated that the temporal lobe processes acoustics, the occipital lobe handles vision, and the frontal lobe manages tactile processing and higher cognitive functions. Sensory perception is a crucial pathway for human interaction with the external environment. However, sensory deficits caused by nervous system damage, disease, or other factors can lead to losing the ability to perceive touch, vision, and hearing.

A significant proportion of the global population has sensory deficits, either congenital or acquired. For instance, in China, nearly 18 million people suffer from visual impairments, accounting for one-fifth of the world's total, and China also has the highest number of individuals with hearing disabilities, totaling 27.8 million. Therefore, addressing the needs of this vast population is of the utmost urgency.

BCI technology aims to establish a communication bridge between the human brain and external devices. Recording and analyzing electrophysiological information like brain signals converts brain activity into machine-readable instructions to control external devices. BCI technology can be applied in several ways to restore lost sensory functions in sensory deficit scenarios.

For patients with lost tactile functions, BCI technology can use implanted electrodes or other sensors to record electrical activities of the brain cortex and then convert these activities into tactile information. With training, patients can learn to perceive tactile stimuli in the external environment through brain signals, effectively recreating the sense of touch. Brain-Machine Touch technology has potential applications ranging from limb perception to skin sensations.

BCI technology can reconstruct visual information for patients with visual impairments using the visual cortex activity. By implanting electrodes or sensors to record brain signals from the visual cortex and then translating these signals into visualized images or patterns, patients can perceive these as visual experiences. This approach is termed Brain-Machine Vision.

BCI technology also plays a role in auditory restoration, known as Brain-Machine Audition. Brain signals can be used to reconstruct sound information for those who have lost hearing. Similarly, electrodes or sensors implanted to record signals from the auditory cortex can translate these signals into sound, providing auditory experiences for patients.

However, BCI technology still faces challenges in sensory restoration. The stability and accuracy of the technology are critical, as precisely parsing and reconstructing complex sensory information requires highly refined decoding of brain signals. Individual differences and adaptation issues may affect the effectiveness of sensory restoration, necessitating personalized training and adjustments. Additionally, ethical and privacy considerations, especially in the use of implantable devices, need thorough attention.

2.1.5 Treating Epilepsy and Neurodevelopmental Disorders

Epilepsy and neurodevelopmental disorders, as neurological conditions, affect the lives of millions worldwide. Epilepsy is a chronic disease caused by abnormal brain electrical activity, while neurodevelopmental disorders encompass a range of conditions affecting the normal growth and functioning of the nervous system. Both conditions pose significant physical and psychological challenges to patients.

There is a close connection between epilepsy and neurodevelopmental disorders. The electrophysiological abnormalities of epileptic seizures are often closely linked to developmental defects in the brain cortex. Hence, BCIs, through recording and analyzing brain waves, hold promise for more accurate diagnosis and treatment of epilepsy.

BCI devices can monitor and record a patient's brain signals in real-time, aiding physicians in understanding the electrophysiological abnormalities of epilepsy. This is crucial for determining the type of epilepsy and the frequency and duration of seizures, thereby laying the foundation for personalized treatment plans. Additionally, BCI technology can provide early warnings before an epileptic seizure, allowing patients and doctors more time to take intervention measures, thus mitigating the severity of the attacks.

Moreover, BCI technology has potential value in the treatment of neurodevelopmental disorders. These disorders can affect the brain's structure and function, leading to issues in perception, motor skills, and social interactions. BCI technology can monitor and analyze patients' brain signals, helping to understand their brain activity patterns and functional states. This information is instrumental in developing personalized rehabilitation plans. Neurofeedback training through brain-machine interfaces (BMIs) can potentially improve neurological functions, enhancing patients' quality of life.

2.2 Mechanical Prostheses: Making Artificial Limbs More Realistic

For years, a primary focus of BCI development has been helping individuals with limb disabilities regain motor function. In the past two decades, scientists have made significant strides in intelligent control of prostheses through decoding neural activities. Given the large number of people with limb disabilities and an aging global population, BCIs have opened a window of hope for this group.

2.2.1 PNS: Wiring Prostheses with Signals

Before BCIs, the best option for those with limb disabilities was fitting prostheses, which were mainly aesthetic and offered limited mobility, struggling with even simple tasks like grasping. By interpreting brain intentions, BCIs have redefined the purpose of prostheses, potentially making them an integral part of the body.

The nervous system is divided into the central and peripheral systems. The central system, composed of the brain and spinal cord, processes information and controls bodily functions. The peripheral system, extending from the spinal cord to the limbs and the rest of the body, facilitates two-way communication with the central system. Our five senses result from neurotransmitter transmissions between neurons in these systems.

In the peripheral system, similar functioning nerves converge into bundles, such as those controlling arm movement. These bundles, varying in diameter from 1–3 millimeters to a centimeter, make it possible to attach or implant microelectrodes.

By recording electrical signals through electrode arrays or microelectrodes on these nerve bundles and processing and decoding this information to relay to prostheses or external devices, individuals with limb disabilities can control these devices or experience sensory information.

Open Bionics, a company that combines 3D printing with electromyography technology, has developed a forearm prosthesis. Attaching electrodes to the skin to detect weak bioelectrical signals from muscle nerve cells allows a degree of autonomous hand positioning and even accomplishes several common gestures for everyday activities.

More impressively, Hugh Herr, a professor from MIT and an amputee himself, has advanced in this area. After losing his legs below the knee due to frostbite during a mountaineering accident, Herr connected his amputated muscles and nerves to a complex bionic prosthesis. This setup restored his walking ability and allowed him to precisely feel his artificial legs' movement and position changes, enabling natural movements like climbing stairs.

Electrodes determine the quality of brain-machine interaction and the "bandwidth" of the BCI. More advanced, precise, and safer electrodes are needed to enhance flexibility and simulate touch. The "Utah Array," proposed by the University of Utah, represents such an advancement in electrode technology.

The Utah Array is a two-dimensional electrode array of silicon known for its durability and stability. Its microarray structure, with electrodes about 1 mm in length and spaced only a few hundred micrometers apart, allows for precise monitoring of neuronal activity. The recording points at the tips of the electrodes enhance signal precision, which is crucial for decoding brain signals into useful control commands. Its high integration capacity, accommodating up to 100 electrodes, covers a broader brain area, providing more data points and ensuring accurate neuronal action potential recording with minimal neural damage. The Utah Array is one of the few BCI electrodes approved by the FDA for human trials and has been successfully implanted for up to two years.

2.2.2 Central Nervous System: Brain-Controlled Prosthetics

For general limb disabilities, reattaching nerves at the amputation site can help patients regain motor and sensory abilities, as these nerves are closely linked to hand or foot movements, simplifying programming. However, for patients with high spinal cord injuries leading to paraplegia, the solution lies in directly extracting information from the brain to convert it into mechanical device control commands. This necessitates using a direct-to-brain BCI, engaging the central nervous system.

The brain's cerebral cortex is divided into different functional areas: frontal, parietal, temporal, and occipital lobes.

1. At the forefront of the cerebral hemispheres, the frontal lobe covers about a third of the brain's surface. It includes several areas responsible for movement, like the motor cortex, and is essential for cognitive functions.
2. The parietal lobe, the sensory center, processes sensory information and aids in focusing attention. Damage here can lead to sensory disorders, spatial disorientation, and body neglect.
3. The temporal lobe deals with auditory processing and is linked to memory, emotions, and psychological functions.
4. The occipital lobe processes visual information, and damage can result in visual disturbances and memory deficits.

The intensity of brainwaves can determine brain wave activity in these areas. Scientists have categorized brainwaves into different rhythms based on frequency, aiding in understanding various brain states.

For instance, alpha waves (7–12 Hz) detected when we relax or close our eyes indicate a relaxed state. Beta waves (12–30 Hz) become prominent during physical activity or even when observing others move, indicating the activation of the brain's "mirror neuron system." Gamma waves (around 40 Hz) are thought to be related to focused attention.

Capturing and manipulating these brainwave changes can enable "mind control" of specific actions. This leads to the concept of "event-related potentials" (ERP). One of the most widely used ERPs in BCIs is the "P300 event-related potential," a significant positive voltage peak around 300 milliseconds after stimulus presentation, often triggered by low-probability events.

The Oddball paradigm, a cognitive psychology experimental setup, exploits this by presenting an infrequent stimulus among frequent ones, like a red shape amid predominantly blue ones. This triggers a P300 response when the rare stimulus appears. The earliest mind-controlled typing systems employed this paradigm. A character matrix is presented to the user, and the rows and columns flash randomly. The user focuses on the desired character's flash, triggering two P300 ERPs and enabling the system to determine the selected character. While this process requires training, once mastered, it enables control of text input purely through thought.

However, applying P300 ERPs demands highly accurate brainwave monitoring and processing due to the subtle differences in timing and amplitude. The BCI system must possess exceptional signal processing and interpretation capabilities for effective user interaction.

The challenge for non-invasive BCIs is the lower signal-to-noise ratio, as the signals aggregate overall brain activity and must pass through the skull and scalp. This limits the functionality to simpler tasks like emotion detection or mechanical human-machine interaction. Invasive electrodes in the brain cortex or deeper receive stronger, less interfered signals. While invasive, for some high-level paralysis patients, this risk is outweighed by the potential benefits of regained mobility.

Cyberkinetics was the first company to implant electrodes in the brain. Using the Utah Array, they developed the "BrainGate" BCI. In 2004, BrainGate was implanted in a 25-year-old quadriplegic patient, Matt Nagle, enabling him to control a computer mouse with his thoughts. By 2012, BrainGate could control a multi-jointed robotic arm, allowing another paralyzed patient, Cathy, to drink a beverage through mind control.

2.2.3 The Walk Again Project: The Paralyzed Soccer Prodigy

A well-known example of BCIs helping paralyzed patients regain mobility is the story of the "soccer prodigy" who kicked the first ball at the 2014 World Cup in Brazil.

In Brazil, where soccer is a cultural phenomenon, almost every young person dreams of playing the sport. Juliano Pinto was no different. However, a tragic car accident shattered his dreams, leaving him with paralysis from the chest down—a condition known as high-level paraplegia. Wheelchair-bound for years, Pinto lost not only the ability to control his lower limbs but also the chance to feel the sensation of touching a soccer ball.

In 2013, Pinto's life took a turn with the Walk Again Project, an international collaborative initiative led by Miguel Nicolelis, a neuroscientist at Duke University. The project brought together neuroscientists, mechanical engineers, and neurorehabilitation experts from around the globe. Nicolelis' ultimate goal was to use technology to enhance the quality of life for paralyzed individuals, and the team's exoskeleton device was key to realizing this vision.

In the winter of 2013, Pinto and seven other paralyzed participants began training with this extraordinary exoskeleton device. Each participant, like Pinto, had lost walking ability due to spinal cord injuries.

The essence of the exoskeleton is BCI technology. Patients wear headgear that collects brain signals, transmitted wirelessly to a computer on their back. The computer then converts these brain signals into movement commands, enabling the exoskeleton to stabilize the body and move the mechanical limbs accordingly. This process, from brain signal emission to exoskeleton movement, takes about 300 milliseconds.

Nicolelis' exoskeleton features sensors at the tip of each mechanical limb, capable of detecting temperature, pressure, and distance—akin to artificial skin. This technology allowed patients, including Pinto, to perform desired movements and regain sensory feedback from their feet.

A year into training with the exoskeleton, Pinto made history at the opening ceremony of the 2014 Brazil World Cup. At São Paulo's Corinthians Stadium, he kicked the tournament's first ball before a crowd of thousands and millions more watching globally. "I felt the soccer ball!" Pinto exclaimed after the successful kick, marking the end of an eight-year journey from paralysis to regaining long-lost sensations.

In 2016, the Nicolelis team published their first clinical report on exoskeleton training, which included improvements in the condition of eight patients, including Pinto. All participants regained some neurological functions previously thought irrecoverable. Pinto could autonomously move his leg muscles and regain sensory perceptions in paralyzed limbs. Others significantly recovered bladder control and cardiovascular functions, substantially enhancing their quality of life.

2.2.4 How Flexible Are Mechanical Prosthetics?

The small step taken by Juliano Pinto at the Brazil World Cup marked a giant leap for BCI technology. A year after this event, in 2015, a young man with a mechanical arm appeared in a Harvard University basement. Following a lab explosion, he tragically lost his right arm. His colleague, Han Bicheng, a PhD student at Harvard's Brain Science Center and leader of the BCI team BrainCo, saw an opportunity to create a prosthetic arm that the brain could control. Although limited in functionality and sensitivity, this brain-controlled mechanical arm was a significant breakthrough.

BrainCo evolved from a research team to an independent BCI company. In 2019, they introduced the world's first brain-controlled mechanical limb, BrainRobotics Smart Bionic Hand. It collects myoelectric signals from amputees' residual limbs and uses deep learning algorithms to interpret their movement intentions, enabling the prosthetic to move in sync with the user's thoughts. This innovation was recognized as one of *Time* magazine's 100 Best Inventions of 2019.

BrainRobotics continued to innovate, launching the Smart Bionic Leg in December 2021. This intelligent prosthesis can collect up to 20,000 myoelectric data points per second, smartly recognizing user intent.

In academia, BCI technology has also made significant breakthroughs in controlling prosthetics for paralyzed patients. In 2015, researchers at the University of Houston developed an EEG-based system that allowed an amputee to control a prosthetic limb to grasp objects like a water cup or credit card.

In 2016, researchers from the University of Minnesota announced a breakthrough in *Scientific Reports*: controlling objects in complex 3D space using thought alone, without brain implants. Using advanced signal processing and machine learning algorithms, they used an EEG cap with 64 electrodes to record brain activity and translate these signals into action.

In 2019, a biomedical engineering team from the University of Utah developed the Utah Slanted Electrode Array, which can be implanted in amputees' forearms. This array translates neural signals into digital commands, allowing the control of mechanical limbs and even providing sensory feedback.

In 2020, a study published in *Science Translational Medicine* by researchers at the University of Michigan revealed a new neural interface technology for precision-controlled prosthetics. They amplified weak signals from the amputees' arm nerves, enabling real-time, precise control of prosthetic fingers.

In 2022, a team from the Johns Hopkins University Applied Physics Laboratory implanted BCIs in both sides of a paralyzed patient's brain, enabling him to use mechanical arms to eat independently. The patient, Robert, paralyzed for over thirty years, underwent a ten-hour surgery to implant six microelectrode arrays in his brain. These arrays collected and analyzed brain signals to control the mechanical arms.

Undoubtedly, achieving rapid, flexible, and smooth control of motor prosthetics through BCI technology is a complex and progressive process. It requires long-term human effort, interdisciplinary collaboration, adventurous volunteers, and sustained societal interest. This process also leads more individuals with limb disabilities to stand and walk again, using this sci-fi-like technology. The human neural motor control system, developed through millions of years of evolution, is a natural "BMI." The complex systems BCIs aim to build represent humanity's second body, continuously updating our understanding of ourselves through this re-creation.

2.3 Reconnecting the Disconnected: BCI's Role in Reestablishing Communication

Beyond aiding mobility, BCIs are pivotal in medical science, particularly in helping patients with fundamental communication barriers reestablish connections with the world. Among these are individuals suffering from locked-in syndrome or ALS, who are nearly completely paralyzed, often communicating only through eye movements. Despite their intact consciousness, they are trapped in non-responsive bodies.

BCIs aim to bring these individuals back into the world.

2.3.1 Thought-to-Text Becomes Reality

Among numerous teams researching BCIs, Frank Willett's group at Stanford University's Howard Hughes Medical Institute stands out. In 2017, they recruited three quadriplegic volunteers, implanting BCIs in their motor cortices. Volunteers imagined using their arms or hands to move cursors, with computers recording and analyzing these brain signals. This allowed them to move cursors on screens and select characters, reaching about 40 characters per minute.

Originally, BCIs were primarily used to restore "motor skills," like controlling mechanical arms to move computer cursors or click letters. Fast forward to 2021, and the same joint team from Howard Hughes Medical Institute and Stanford University made a significant leap in BCI development. They decoded brain activity related to "handwritten" thoughts, enabling paralyzed individuals to type without using their hands.

They developed an intracortical BCI system that decoded neural activity from imagined handwriting movements, using recurrent neural networks (RNNs) to convert these movements into text in real-time. Remarkably, a paralyzed participant typed about 90 characters per minute, more than double the previous BCI typing record, with an initial accuracy of 94.1% and an offline accuracy exceeding 99% after auto-correction.

One participant, known as T5, who had participated in the earlier study, suffered from spinal cord injury resulting in quadriplegia. In the new study, electrodes implanted in his brain's areas controlling right-hand and arm movements captured neuronal signals. These were then transmitted to a computer. The research first confirmed that the brain's neural activity could still represent the writing process despite years without physical writing.

Every English character has a unique shape and writing speed, making the neural activity for each character distinct. The researchers used nonlinear dimensionality reduction (t-SNE) for two-dimensional visualization of neural activity clusters for each trial, showing distinct clusters for different characters and movement encoding processes.

The next step involved the RNN, which transformed neural activity into character probabilities. T5 had to write sentences, including 26 lowercase letters and punctuation. The RNN was trained with neural activity data collected as T5 imagined writing, creating a data set of over 31,000 characters in 7.6 hours.

The RNN gradually learned to distinguish the brain signals corresponding to different letters. In practical tests, T5 could type about 18 words or 90 characters per minute, nearly reaching the average smartphone typing speed of 115 characters per minute. Even in free-response tasks, his input reached about 73.8 characters per minute.

While not perfect, the neural algorithm's accuracy was impressive. For copied sentences, there was about one error every 18–19 characters, and in free composition, one error every 11–12 characters. Like smartphone autocorrect features, an error-correction algorithm applied to BCI reduced the error rate to about 1%.

This advancement in BCI technology is a monumental step in enabling individuals with severe communication impairments to engage in near-normal typing activities, effectively opening new avenues for interaction and expression. As BCIs evolve, they promise to unlock new realms of communication for those who have long been isolated by physical limitations, transforming their interactions with the world around them.

2.3.2 Empowering the Speech-Impaired to "Speak" through BCIs

In addition to enabling paralyzed patients to write through thought, a groundbreaking advancement in 2022 from the Howard Hughes Medical Institute and Stanford University's joint team introduced a novel BCI that converts neural activities related to speech into text. This voice BCI, the first to transcribe speech from cortical microelectrode array recordings, offers a voice to those silenced by strokes, ALS, also known as Lou Gehrig's disease, and similar ailments.

How Does It Help Stroke and ALS Patients "Speak"?

We know that the brain communicates through electrical signals between neurons. When we speak, specific neurons become active, creating what's known as neural activity. These signals appear in different ways at different times. The research team captured these activities and translated them into words, allowing those with speech impairments to communicate with the world.

Tiny electrodes implanted in patients' brains recorded this neural activity, functioning like miniature monitors inside the brain. Scientists then employed decoding algorithms to process these signals. The process resembled translation: merging and smoothing signals from various electrodes into a coherent "musical melody." Then, using a technique called RNNs, the team transformed these time-sequenced neural signals into probabilities for each phoneme, the smallest units of sound in speech.

But speaking involves more than just phonemes; it requires forming meaningful sentences. To achieve this, the team combined phoneme probabilities with a vast language model, understanding which phonemes form coherent words and sentences. Ultimately, this system translated patients' brain activity into text, displayed on screens, or vocalized. This development allowed speech-impaired individuals to communicate through text, a significant step forward.

This BCI enabled patients with language impairments to communicate at a rate of 62 words per minute, approaching the speed of natural conversation. It meant that those who had lost the ability to speak could reintegrate into social and daily life, bringing new hope and opportunities.

BCI's Rapid Progress in Communication

In 2023, two studies in *Nature* highlighted breakthroughs in using invasive BCIs, allowing severely paralyzed individuals to communicate with unprecedented accuracy and speed. These independent studies showcased different BCI designs from the teams of Stanford University and the University of California-San Francisco.

Stanford's team developed a BCI device with tiny electrode arrays implanted in the brain, collecting individual neuronal activities and decoding them with artificial neural networks. Their BCI enabled an ALS patient to communicate 62 words per minute, a 3.4-fold increase from previous devices, nearing normal speech speed. The device handled a vocabulary of 12,500 words, a significant breakthrough despite a higher error rate.

The UCSF team's device, with electrodes covering the brain's surface, captured multiple cells' activities, converting brain signals into text, voice, and avatar control. Their deep learning model decoded neural data from a stroke patient attempting to form silent sentences. The system converted brain signals into text at 78 words per minute with a 25% error rate, which increased as the vocabulary expanded.

Significant differences in implant design existed between the two studies. Stanford used cortical microarrays (Utah arrays), while UCSF employed larger ECoG electrodes (cortical brain electrodes) used for epilepsy surgery patients.

Stanford's device, implanted in the patient's cortical areas, used tiny silicon electrodes in square arrays. Each array had 64 electrodes, with 128 microelectrodes spaced as thin as half the thickness of a credit card. UCSF's device placed a paper-thin rectangular array with 253 electrodes over brain areas related to facial movements. Each electrode captured thousands of neurons' activities.

The UCSF team trained AI algorithms with the volunteer's participation to recognize brain signals associated with phonemes. The training involved phrases from a vocabulary of 1,024 words until the computer recognized patterns of brain activity for all basic speech sounds. They also animated the volunteer's avatar using software from a company specializing in AI-driven facial animation. The team created custom machine learning workflows for this software, combining them with the volunteers' brain signals when attempting to speak and transforming them into facial movements.

These advancements in BCI technology have opened new avenues for those imprisoned within their bodies due to neurological conditions to reengage in normal communication, offering them a chance that was previously unimaginable. As Debara Tucci from the National Institute on Deafness and Other Communication Disorders rightly pointed out, "Communication is key to societal functioning," BCIs undoubtedly offer a lifeline for reestablishing these essential connections.

2.4 The Pursuit of Happiness: A Neurological Approach

In our modern world, attaining happiness can be a daunting challenge. The tragic passing of Chinese American singer Coco Lee reignited discussions on depression, a prevalent mental health issue worldwide. According to the World Health Organization, depression is a leading global mental disorder, impacting life quality more severely than heart disease or cancer. Currently, an estimated 350 million people are suffering from depression globally, with about one million annual suicides. The financial burden of mental disorders is projected to reach a staggering US$16 trillion by 2030. In China alone, the number of people suffering from depression has soared to 95 million.

Depression traps its sufferers in a cycle of persistent sadness, self-denial, and a lack of interest or energy. The ambiguity surrounding its causes and lengthy treatment processes only adds to the fear and stigma associated with it. Traditional treatments like medication and psychotherapy often fall short for many, particularly those with treatment-resistant depression (TRD), which affects over 30% of patients.

2.4.1 Optimal Solution for Treating Depression

BCIs offer a novel and seemingly optimal solution for treating depression. As author Andrew Solomon, with his three-decade-long battle with depression, describes in *The Noonday Demon*, there's nothing simple about the chemical processes in the brain. From the sunlight to the hardness of rocks, from the taste of seawater to the nostalgia evoked by a spring breeze, all boil down to chemistry.

Despite attributing depression to aberrant chemical reactions in the brain, the connection between these physical processes and our thoughts or feelings remains unclear. With 12 billion neurons and countless rapidly changing synapses in the human brain, our understanding still needs to be completed. The brain houses numerous neurotransmitters, and influencing one can inadvertently affect another, impacting bodily functions. Psychological counseling, pharmaceuticals, and physical therapies like electroconvulsive therapy all aim to recalibrate these internal chemical movements to achieve a semblance of balance.

BCI as a Beacon of Hope

BCIs, which involve monitoring brain activity and decoding neural signals into computer commands, present new hope for depression treatment. They connect the patient's brain to an external computer or device, monitoring and regulating brain activity to alleviate symptoms.

BCIs monitor brain electrical signals using EEG, fMRI, or MEG. By analyzing these signals, researchers can identify brain areas and patterns linked to depression, such as reduced prefrontal cortex activity and heightened amygdala activity. Once depression-related patterns are identified, BCIs can provide real-time brain feedback, aiding patients in understanding their brain state. Furthermore, BCIs can intervene with neurofeedback training, adjusting brain activity patterns.

Some BCI systems can even directly modulate brain activity non-invasively through transcranial direct current stimulation (tDCS) or transcranial magnetic stimulation (TMS), restoring normal brain activity patterns.

BCI treatments are highly personalized, catering to patients' unique brain activity patterns. This indicates that BCIs could be a more targeted and effective treatment, offering individualized assistance.

Promising Outcomes

Studies have shown hopeful outcomes of BCI treatments for depression. A 2018 study in *Translational Psychiatry* demonstrated positive results, with 23 moderate-to-severe depression patients showing significant improvement after six weeks of BCI treatment, which persisted for six months post-treatment.

Another study in the journal *Nature Human Behavior* in 2020 found effective relief in some participants with TRD after 12 weeks of BCI treatment. Seven of the ten participants showed notable symptom reduction, with four achieving complete remission.

The transformations experienced by individuals undergoing BCI treatment for depression are profound. Many struggle with despair and an inability to control their symptoms. However, BCI treatments can empower individuals to manage their symptoms better, boosting their capabilities and confidence.

In some cases, it can even completely alleviate depressive symptoms, allowing individuals to regain their quality of life and resume normal activities.

Beyond psychological benefits, BCI treatments can positively impact physical health. Depression often correlates with inflammation and other physiological changes, increasing the risk of other health issues like cardiovascular diseases. By reducing depressive symptoms, BCI treatments can also help mitigate inflammation and other physiological changes related to depression, thereby improving overall health.

2.4.2 The "Happiness Switch": A Technological Breakthrough

The end of 2020 marked the beginning of a revolutionary project at Shanghai's Ruijin Hospital, tackling TRD with BCI technology. This pioneering clinical trial, "BCI Neuro-regulation for the Treatment of TRD," involved 26 patients. The results, published in 2023, showed an average improvement in depressive symptoms of over 60%. The participants, some of whom shared their remarkable experiences, underwent a transformative journey.

The trial's experimental principle was groundbreaking. It involved surgically implanting a "brain pacemaker" in the patient's chest and inserting two electrodes into the brain. The pacemaker activated the electrodes by an external switch, instantly elevating the patient's mood. Post-surgery, with medical guidance, patients found their optimal neural stimulation pattern. They could regulate their mood using a programmer (a device for adjusting stimulation parameters) and a smartphone app.

The app featured three modes: work, rest, and leisure. The work mode simulated a normal state, while the rest mode, akin to a low-stimulation setting, reverted patients to a depressive state. The leisure mode's intensity was intermediate. Each mode switch stimulated a new target in the brain, avoiding tolerance development.

From a neuroscientific perspective, the brain pacemaker stimulates the frontal neural nuclei with electric currents, diminishing depressive symptoms by significantly increasing dopamine levels. This was corroborated by biochemical and biophysical evidence regarding neurotransmitters.

A double-blind method was employed to ensure the trial's integrity and the patients' authenticity: the assessment team evaluated patient conditions. In contrast, the control team managed the program switches or shutdowns. This meant that the assessing doctors were unaware of whether the patient's device was on or at what stimulation level, and the patients themselves were unaware of their stimulation status, thus serving as controls.

Patient responses to electrical stimulation varied. Some felt little during the trial, while others, more sensitive, experienced clearer sensations of happiness.

One of the participants, 31-year-old Wu Xiaotian, had suffered from depression for 16 years. At his worst, he lay motionless in bed all day, unable to utter even a simple greeting. In January 2022, Wu opted for Ruijin Hospital's clinical trial. The surgery was in two stages: first, small holes were drilled in the skull to fix electrodes to the brain's cortex, then sealed with special material. Days later, the second stage involved extending the cortical electrodes to the chest, connecting them to the deep brain stimulation (DBS) brain pacemaker/electromagnetic pulse generator implanted in the chest. Three days post-surgery, Wu's crucial moment of "switching on" arrived. "It wasn't as scary as imagined. There was no discomfort, just an instant feeling of clarity and happiness," he recalled. Wu noted the need for adjustments post-surgery. Initially, the calm and pleasant sensations began to fade, and depressive feelings loomed. The hospital remotely adjusted parameters, which temporarily improved his mood. Eventually, Wu was given control over the settings via an app on his phone.

Wu, one of the more neurologically sensitive patients, showed significant differences in his state before and after implantation. Dr. Sun Bomin, director of Functional Neurosurgery and the BCI Neuro-regulation Center at Ruijin, supported Wu's proposal for self-regulation. The app allowed Wu to switch between work (normal state), rest (depressive state), and leisure (intermediate intensity) modes, stimulating new brain targets each time to prevent tolerance.

Over a year, Wu's depression significantly improved. Managing a bed-and-breakfast suits his sociable nature, and his singing has improved with each performance. Dr. Sun confirmed a 90% improvement in Wu's depression.

Another participant, "Brother Tang," experienced his device's activation in 2021. The process was calm, with doctors continuously making adjustments. Tang, diagnosed with depression and suffering from insomnia for years, hoped the technology would grant him a good night's sleep—his greatest wish at over 40 years old.

Not every participant experienced such dramatic effects, but overall improvements were significant. Dr. Sun stated that among the 23 patients enrolled, depressive symptoms improved by over 60% on average. "For TRD, a 60% improvement rate is remarkable," he said.

This innovative application of BCI in treating depression represents a significant stride in mental health care. It offers hope to millions suffering silently, marking a new era where technology bridges the gap between human experience and medical intervention.

2.4.3 Brain Digital Pills: A New Frontier in Depression Treatment

In January 2023, Inner Cosmos, a leading BCI company, introduced a groundbreaking device for treating depression: the "Brain Digital Pill." This micro-implant, akin to a cochlear implant, holds promise for addressing other cognitive disorders in the future. Already implanted in the first patient's skull for depression treatment, Inner Cosmos is eagerly anticipating the start of their second human trial. Initially unveiled in St. Louis, Missouri, this technology will undergo a year-long evaluation.

The Brain Digital Pill is recognized as the smallest and least invasive technology to date, with the implant no larger than a penny. It comprises two components: an electrode under the scalp and a "prescription box" clipped to the hair for powering the device. The implant, the size of a fingernail, is inconspicuously placed under the skin near the skull. The "prescription box," small enough to clip onto hair, provides power remotely, eliminating the need for a clinician's physical presence. The implant sends daily 15-minute pulses to the left dorsolateral prefrontal cortex, an area affected by depression. Clinicians can monitor the patient's brain status in real-time via a dashboard. Notably, the external device need not be worn when not in treatment.

2.4.4 The Ethics of the "Happiness Switch"

As with any novel technology, widespread adoption of BCI for depression treatment necessitates addressing ethical concerns. How should we perceive this emotion-regulating breakthrough? Would you be willing to implant a happiness switch in your brain?

First, the innovation of this technology is undeniable. BCIs, as a new medical device, are garnering increasing attention. Apart from aiding physically disabled patients, BCIs offer breakthroughs in mental health treatment. Since traditional therapies, like cognitive-behavioral therapy and pharmacotherapy, are not universally effective and require continuous application to prevent relapse, BCIs might herald a new era in treating depression. Moreover, these technologies can deepen our understanding of depression's mechanisms.

Currently, BCIs are trialed on severe cases where medications have failed. Many patients, hoping for relief, are turning to BCIs. Results from Ruijin Hospital's clinical trials have been promising, with some patients regaining the sensation of happiness.

Beyond treating depression, BCIs can target other specific neural sites in the brain to address various neurological disorders, like bipolar disorder and schizophrenia. By stimulating specific motor neurons in the brain, BCIs can effectively regulate emotional feedback.

However, broader application raises questions about free will, the pursuit of happiness, and self-determination. When using BCIs for happiness, we must consider the balance between short-term and long-term well-being and the potential risks and abuse. Additionally, perceptions of depression and happiness vary, raising concerns about the potential misuse of BCIs as a new form of "electronic drug."

Data privacy and security are also critical. BCIs collect sensitive neural data, necessitating stringent standards and regulatory mechanisms to protect patient privacy.

Further research is needed to establish the long-term efficacy of BCIs in treating depression and their potential to help specific patient subsets, like those with TRD.

While BCIs in treating depression are still in the early stages, their potential benefits are immense. Depression is a complex and multifaceted illness, and no one-size-fits-all treatment exists. BCIs could offer a novel, innovative approach to treating depression tailored to individual brain activity patterns.

As a promising and innovative method for treating depression and other mental health disorders, BCIs hold the potential to revolutionize the field of mental health, bringing hope to millions battling this debilitating condition. Continuous research and investment may one day make BCIs the treatment of choice for depression, improving overall health and bringing high-quality life and well-being to many.

2.5 The Synergy of Digital Therapeutics and Brain-Computer Interfaces

Imagine a future where a visit to the doctor for an ailment results in a prescription not for medication but for a software application, with the advice to "play it for 15 minutes a day." This seemingly baffling scenario could soon become a reality in clinics, thanks to digital therapeutics—an innovative treatment modality from digital technology. With the advent of BCIs, digital therapeutics are poised to revolutionize healthcare.

2.5.1 What Is Digital Therapeutics?

The concept of digital therapeutics dates back to 1995 when Dr. Joseph Kvedar in Boston spearheaded a project to establish a "one-to-many" medical service technology system distinct from traditional clinical approaches. This initiative laid the groundwork for what would be known as digital therapeutics. In 2010, the FDA approved the first digital therapeutic product.

By 2012, the concept had gained traction in the US. The Digital Therapeutics Alliance defines digital therapeutics as evidence-based, software-driven intervention programs designed to treat, manage, or prevent diseases. These solutions can be used independently or with medications, devices, or other therapies.

In simpler terms, where traditional treatments involve patients receiving medication prescribed by a doctor, digital therapeutics replace the medication with software applications or a combination of software and hardware. These can range from gamified programs to behavior guidance plans, all aimed at inducing biological changes at the cellular or even molecular level, thereby impacting the disease state.

Digital therapeutics include "active digital ingredients" and "digital excipients," akin to their pharmaceutical counterparts. The "active ingredients" are responsible for the clinical benefits. At the same time, the "excipients" encompass elements like virtual assistants, natural language processing systems, digital incentive schemes, and communication tools with doctors and other patients.

For instance, a patient suffering from chronic insomnia might traditionally receive medication like sedatives or undergo face-to-face Cognitive Behavioral Therapy for Insomnia (CBT-I). Digital therapeutics like the FDA-approved Somryst® bring this therapy online, overcoming limitations of time and space. Somryst® includes a sleep log and six instructional modules, guiding patients to establish good sleep habits over a nine-week course.

Digital therapeutics offer clear advantages in today's Internet era. They allow remote implementation of consultation or treatment, reducing unnecessary hospital visits, which was especially relevant during the pandemic. They can be personalized according to the patient's time and physical space constraints and are easily scalable through smartphones or tablets.

In digital therapeutics, BCIs open innovative and personalized treatment opportunities. BCIs can tailor treatment plans by monitoring a patient's brain signals and individual physiological differences, ensuring more targeted therapy for each individual. This means patients receive treatments matched to their specific needs and conditions, enhancing the effectiveness of the therapy.

BCIs also enable real-time monitoring of physiological and neurological states, dynamically adjusting treatment plans. This ensures that therapies always adapt to the patient's condition, enhancing efficacy and safety. For mental health issues, BCIs can monitor emotional states for timely intervention. In neurorehabilitation, BCIs can control external devices, improving rehabilitation outcomes.

Additionally, BCIs make digital therapeutics more sustainable. Patients can use digital therapies at home with professional support without frequent hospital or clinic visits. This improves the accessibility of treatments and reduces healthcare costs.

Combining digital therapeutics and BCIs represents a new frontier in digital technology innovations, offering exciting possibilities for future healthcare. With these advancements, the once-unimaginable treatment modalities are becoming a reality, heralding a new era in personalized and effective medical care.

2.5.2 A Medical Paradigm Revolution: The Fusion of Digital Therapeutics and Brain-Computer Interfaces

The greatest significance of integrating digital therapeutics with BCIs lies in technological breakthroughs and in revolutionizing medication. This transformation reshapes our approach to disease treatment, offering more effective methods to combat various ailments.

Mental Health Treatment

One of the most prolific applications of digital therapeutics lies in mental health treatment. From depression, ADHD, and cognitive disorders in the elderly to schizophrenia, digital therapeutics have shown promising results.

For instance, the FDA has approved a technique that uses video games to treat ADHD in young adults, marking it as the world's first game-based digital therapeutic. Akili, a notable US digital therapeutics company, has extended its reach beyond ADHD to alleviate symptoms of autism and memory decline in the elderly. A study involving 169 participants showed significant improvements in attention span in adolescents after using this game-based therapy.

In the realm of autism spectrum disorders, the combination of digital therapeutics and BCIs has been particularly impactful. BrainCo's StarKids, a child-focused BCI training system, offers precision closed-loop neurofeedback training to improve core brain function and behavioral deficits in children with developmental delays, enhancing social cognition and motivation.

For depression and anxiety, the combination of digital therapeutics and BCIs shows a promising future. Unlike traditional therapies that rely on verbal or written expressions of emotions, BCIs can directly monitor brain activity for a more accurate assessment of emotional states. This allows for immediate adjustment of therapeutic content based on real-time data, offering instant support without waiting for a clinician's intervention.

Cancer Treatment

In cancer treatment, traditional methods involve surgical removal of tumors, complemented by radiation, chemotherapy, or targeted drugs. Digital therapeutics and BCIs have the potential to offer more personalized and effective treatment options. These technologies can provide immediate feedback to improve symptom management by monitoring physiological and emotional states. They can also deliver personalized treatments based on the patient's physiological condition and disease response.

Chronic Disease Management

Chronic diseases provide a broad scope for digital therapeutics and BCIs. These lifestyle diseases, often resulting from poor habits, can be better managed through behavior modification, a key feature of digital therapeutics. Continuous glucose monitoring in diabetes management, for instance, creates digital biomarkers that reflect a patient's physiological and emotional states. This data can guide personalized interventions, improving treatment outcomes.

In summary, the convergence of digital therapeutics and BCIs represents a paradigm shift in healthcare, heralding a revolution in medical treatment. It promises to deliver more efficient, high-quality, low-cost, and accessible medical solutions, effectively treating a wider range of diseases. As this field continues to evolve, we can anticipate a more effective approach to healthcare, transforming the medical landscape significantly.

CHAPTER 3

THE INFINITE POSSIBILITIES OF BRAIN-COMPUTER INTERFACES

3.1 Journey toward the Ultimate in Intelligent Interaction

3.1.1 Evolution of Interaction Modes

Since the advent of computing, human-computer interaction (HCI) has significantly evolved, moving from basic command-line interfaces to the current sophisticated systems. This progression reflects humanity's relentless pursuit of more intuitive and natural ways to interact with machines.

In the early days, interaction with computers was rudimentary, using punch cards to input data. These massive machines required manual translation of problems into binary language, punched into paper tapes, and read by the computer. This time-consuming process could have been more efficient without direct interaction between humans and machines.

However, the information revolution brought HCI into sharp focus. As Internet technology developed, interaction design borrowed from traditional industrial design gained importance. This shift aligned with a growing emphasis on user experience and usability. During this era, we witnessed a transition from character-user interfaces to graphical user interfaces (GUIs).

Keyboard interaction, familiar to most, involves entering specific commands to execute algorithms, with results displayed on a screen. The mouse-drag interaction, developed by Xerox PARC (Palo Alto Research Center) in 1972 for their Xerox PARC computer, introduced a mouse to control the GUI. This innovation led to the concepts of windows, menus, and icons, allowing direct computer manipulation in a more human-centric way.

A significant leap in HCI occurred on January 9, 2007, with the release of Apple's first iPhone, ushering in the era of touchscreen interaction. This marked a paradigm shift from keyboard and mouse interactions to a more intuitive touch-based interface. Around this time, mobile phones evolved to rival personal computers in capabilities, blurring the line between these devices. Touchscreen interaction eliminated the need for learning specific commands, enabling natural interactions through touch, gestures, facial expressions, and voice.

Over nearly four decades, we have maximized the exploration of HCI methods. Yet, with technological advancements, HCI is poised for another revolutionary leap driven by BCIs. BCIs are emerging as a new mode of HCI, offering unprecedented interaction experiences and signifying another groundbreaking shift in how humans interact with machines.

3.1.2 The Ultimate Mode of Human-Machine Interaction

BMIs: Bridging Human Thought and Technology

The human brain, a complex hub of thoughts, emotions, perceptions, actions, and memories, endows us with unique intelligence and individuality. Recent advances in neuroscience, encompassing molecular and cellular studies, key components, software and hardware development, application systems, and instrumentation, have paved the way for the commercial application of BMIs. In this context, BMIs are increasingly recognized as a novel and ultimate mode of interaction between humans and machines.

Why BMIs Represent the Pinnacle of Interaction

BMIs create a pathway for information exchange between the organic brain and devices capable of processing or computing, effectively removing intermediaries in traditional human-machine interactions. This direct connection is precisely why BMIs are considered the ultimate interaction method.

Traditionally, human-machine interaction relies on external input devices like keyboards, mice, and touchscreens to convey human intentions and instructions to computers. Despite advancements over the decades, these devices have limitations in speed, accuracy, naturalness, and accessibility. More critically, they require the translation of brain impulses into physical expressions, often leading to losing information during this conversion process. In contrast, BMIs operate on a fundamentally different principle: they read brain signals and convert human thoughts and intentions directly into computer commands. This direct brain-to-computer connection offers unparalleled advantages over traditional interaction methods.

Advantages of BMIs over Traditional Interfaces

1. Elimination of Physical Actions. BMIs remove the need for physical actions required by traditional input devices, making them revolutionary for individuals with limited or lost physical capabilities. This means controlling computers and external devices solely through thought, enhancing the quality of life and independence of those with disabilities.

2. Universal Applicability. Unlike traditional interfaces that depend on specific physical or linguistic abilities, BMIs can be used across various age groups, cultural backgrounds, and disability levels. This broad applicability opens new possibilities in healthcare, special education, and social integration, making digital society more inclusive.

3. Speed and Response Time. BMIs significantly outpace traditional input devices in speed and responsiveness. While keyboards and mice require complex actions for input or commands, BMIs can instantly capture and execute user intentions, which is crucial for precision-demanding applications like medical surgeries, military operations, and immersive virtual reality experiences.

4. Natural Interaction. BMIs align with the natural human process of thinking and speaking. Traditional devices often require additional learning and adaptation, but BMIs' directness makes them more intuitive, reducing the learning curve and cognitive load associated with interaction.

As we journey through the evolution of human-machine interaction, BMIs stand at the forefront of this new phase, offering transformative possibilities for human life and productivity. They signify a technological leap and a paradigm shift in our approach to integrating our thoughts directly with the digital realm. BMIs are set to redefine the interaction landscape, bridging the gap between human cognition and machine capability in previously unimaginable ways.

3.1.3 Mind-Controlled Smart Homes: The Future of Interaction

Harnessing Thought for Intelligent Home Automation

As the ultimate form of human-machine interaction, BMIs vastly expand the possibilities for smart homes, promising a future where our thoughts can control our living environment.

Current Smart Homes: Lacking True Intelligence

Today's smart homes are essentially traditional mechanical controls repackaged with a layer of interactivity. Most interactions require manual inputs, transitioning from mechanical switches to touchscreen gestures or integrated voice commands. However, these interfaces fall short of the envisioned truly intelligent home environment—a space that understands and responds to our thoughts without any physical interaction.

The Ideal Smart Home Powered by BMIs

The smart home of our imagination is a living space that responds instantly to our mental commands. Imagine a scenario where controlling lights, air conditioning, curtains, windows, sound systems, and televisions requires nothing more than a fleeting thought. This is what true intelligent home automation looks like—a vision made increasingly attainable with the advancement of BMIs.

BMIs: Transforming Home Interactions

BMIs can measure and interpret central nervous system signals to control external home devices, creating a feedback loop that integrates human cognition with intelligent systems. This integration allows for a nuanced understanding and enhancement of neural interactions with our living environment. With BMIs, our homes will understand, interpret, and execute our thoughts, leading to a new level of personalized automation.

The Role of BMIs in Home Automation

BMIs can act as "remote controls," enabling us to operate lights, doors, curtains, and even home service robots with our minds. This technology offers the following:

1. Direct Control of Home Devices. BMIs allow for seamless control of household appliances like lights, TVs, and sound systems through mere thoughts, bypassing physical or vocal commands. Imagine changing TV channels or adjusting volume simply by focusing on your intent.
2. Personalized Environmental Customization. BMIs can tailor the home environment to individual preferences, enhancing comfort and efficiency. For instance, the system could adjust lighting and temperature to suit different family members or use environmental adjustments to help reduce stress levels.
3. Improved Sleep Quality. BMIs can detect and adjust brainwave patterns conducive to sleep, potentially improving conditions like insomnia. The technology could dynamically adjust bedding and environmental factors, such as scent release or gentle vibrations, to aid in falling asleep.

The Future of Intelligent Homes with BMIs

BMIs promise a future where homes respond to our basic commands and anticipate and adapt to our needs and preferences. This technology will redefine smart homes, offering unprecedented convenience, comfort, and energy efficiency. As BMIs become more integrated into our living spaces, they will significantly enhance our quality of life, turning homes into brilliant environments that resonate with our thoughts and desires. The rise of BMIs in home automation is a technological marvel and a step toward a more human-centric and responsive living experience.

3.2 Redefining Future Education with BMIs

A Revolutionary Leap beyond AI in Education

The impact of AI on education, significant as it is, pales in comparison to the transformative potential of BMI technology. Emerging from recent break-throughs in neuroscience, BMIs can interpret brain signals and convert them into actions, facilitating a more natural form of human-machine interaction. This opens new frontiers and challenges in educational technology applications.

Unlocking Educational Opportunities with BMIs

As BMI technology matures, its ability to access and interpret the brain's internal mechanisms is becoming a valuable source of rich educational data. This data can enhance school education and classroom learning by providing convenient tools and technical support for designing learning environments, recording learning processes, and analyzing learning behaviors. Most notably, BMI technology is poised to fundamentally and permanently alter how humans learn.

A Paradigm Shift in Learning

BMIs offer a profound shift in learning modalities by integrating the reading and writing capabilities of the human brain with AI and online technologies. This integration could turn human memory into a computer hard drive, where storage and rewriting of memories and knowledge are possible. The focus of human learning will no longer be limited to the brain's capacity to store information. Still, it will expand to include how effectively we can interface with and manipulate this information.

The Impact of BMIs on Memory and Knowledge

The potential of BMIs to store and rewrite memory will redefine the nature of learning and knowledge acquisition. Traditional learning methods rely heavily on the brain's ability to memorize and recall information, which is often time-consuming and limited by individual capacity. With BMIs, the storage of memories and knowledge can be externalized, allowing for instant access and modification. This shift could lead to a dramatic increase in the speed and efficiency of learning, enabling learners to acquire and process information at unprecedented rates.

Implications for Educational Practices and Systems

The advent of BMI technology in education will necessitate reevaluating current educational practices and systems. As the need for rote memorization diminishes, the focus of education may shift toward developing critical thinking, creativity, and problem-solving skills. Additionally, BMIs could democratize learning by providing equal access to information and learning tools, regardless of a learner's innate cognitive abilities or socioeconomic background.

Challenges and Considerations

Despite its transformative potential, the integration of BMI technology in education will face several challenges. Ethical considerations regarding data privacy, security, and the potential for misuse must be addressed. There will also be a need to develop standardized protocols and guidelines to ensure the safe and equitable use of BMIs in educational settings.

Conclusion: A New Era of Learning

BMI technology stands at the forefront of a new era in education, offering exciting possibilities for enhanced learning and knowledge acquisition. As we navigate the challenges and explore the full potential of this technology, we are on the cusp of redefining what it means to learn and know in the 21st century.

The future of education with BMIs promises a more integrated, efficient, and inclusive learning experience, opening new horizons for learners worldwide.

3.2.1 The Window of Observation: Harnessing BMI in Education

Evaluating Cognitive States in Learning

The influence of cognitive states such as emotional conditions, levels of concentration, and cognitive load on learning processes and outcomes is widely recognized. Positive emotions like excitement and joy can spur learners' interest and active participation, fostering better knowledge absorption and retention. In contrast, negative emotions such as anxiety and stress may lead to distraction and worry, negatively impacting learning outcomes.

Attention Span: The Bedrock of Learning

Attention span is another critical factor affecting learning outcomes. The renowned Italian educator Maria Montessori once said, "Attention is the basis of all learning." A higher concentration level equates to more efficient learning and quicker academic improvement. Conversely, a lack of focus can lead to diminished learning outcomes. This is because concentration is closely linked to information processing capabilities. Learning involves absorbing, processing, and memorizing vast amounts of information. A student's level of concentration directly influences their ability to process information. They are more likely to concentrate on the task and better understand and absorb the content when focused. However, a scattered attention span can lead to missed or incomplete information processing, affecting learning outcomes.

Cognitive Load: Managing Information Processing

Cognitive load refers to the cognitive resources required to perform a specific task. In learning, students must process information, including new concepts, facts, and relationships. When the cognitive load of a learning task is optimal, students can effectively understand and absorb this information, enhancing learning outcomes. However, an excessive cognitive load can overwhelm students, making it difficult to cope with tasks and leading to missed or confused information, thus reducing learning effectiveness.

The Significance of BMIs

BMIs offer a unique means to monitor and measure individual brain electrical activity, physiological signals, or brain imaging data. This technology provides educational researchers and educators with deeper insights and tools to improve learning processes and outcomes.

For instance, in monitoring emotional states, BMI technology can help determine an individual's emotional experiences by monitoring brain physiological activity, such as EEG or fMRI. Certain brainwave patterns or brain region activities associated with different emotional states enable educators to better understand students' emotional states and provide emotional support or intervention as needed.

BMI technology is also instrumental in monitoring and assessing students' concentration levels. Analysis of brain electrical activity or physiological signals can determine whether students are highly focused. For example, focused states usually accompany certain brainwave patterns that indicate whether students are attentive to learning tasks. If concentration levels drop, educators can take measures to help students refocus, thus enhancing learning effectiveness.

BMI technology's individualized, real-time, and situational attributes provide unique advantages in its application in education. First, BMI technology is committed to precisely recognizing individual intentions and states, aligning with the recent trend of personalized learning in education. Additionally, the technology's "online" characteristic, i.e., real-time analysis and output during task execution, offers timely feedback and intervention for practical teaching needs. Moreover, BMI technology aims to be used in everyday settings outside the laboratory, already impacting football fields, stages, classrooms, and more.

This means that even before BMIs achieve deep integration with human brain reading and writing, educators can still use BMI technology to monitor students' attention levels. Integrating with AI technology, educators can allocate learning tasks based on fluctuations in attention levels. This new approach in educational practice promises a more dynamic and responsive learning environment, where teaching methods adapt to students' cognitive states, thereby enhancing the overall effectiveness and quality of education.

3.2.2 Real-Time Recognition of Learning States: The Role of BMIs

The Emergence of BMI in Education

BMIs have made significant strides in education, particularly in the real-time recognition and monitoring of learning states. This application involves collecting neurophysiological activities of students in typical learning scenarios and using machine learning and deep learning techniques to provide real-time monitoring, identification, feedback, and intervention in the learning process.

Utilizing EEG Systems for Monitoring Learning States

Researchers have employed BMI technology, particularly EEG systems, to monitor and tag learners' states while engaging in Massive Open Online Courses and watching online videos. EEG, a non-invasive method for recording brain electrical activity, places electrodes on the scalp to capture spontaneous brain activity over time. This method has proven effective in fostering self-awareness about their learning states among learners, thereby improving academic performance.

Enhancing Teacher-Student Collaboration

Recognizing psychological states through EEG systems can facilitate effective collaboration between teachers and students, improving learning outcomes. In an emotion-based learning system, the NeuroSky brainwave visualizer is used for concentration and relaxation training. This system automatically records negative emotional states when detected, halting teaching activities and logging effective learning time in the database. Additionally, the system can offer games to help learners relax and stabilize negative emotions, thereby improving their learning mood and helping them regain focus for continued learning.

Focus Levels: A Key Cognitive State in Learning

Concentration levels are the most emphasized cognitive state in learning scenarios involving BMIs. These interfaces can read students' attention indices during learning and use neurofeedback training to enhance their concentration. Research indicates that changes in attention are closely linked to theta, alpha, and beta waves. One can accurately reflect the state of attention by analyzing the ratios of different brainwave bands in EEG signals. With precise feedback from brainwaves and neurofeedback training, enhancement of brain functions becomes achievable.

Neurofeedback Training: Enhancing Brain Functions

Since the 1970s, organizations like NASA have used neurofeedback training to enhance astronauts' focus during space missions, reducing errors in space work. Similarly, in education, the attention index is a reliable teaching assessment tool, accurately reflecting participants' focus levels in classrooms. Neurofeedback training for concentration is expected to boost learners' efficiency significantly.

Commercial Applications of Non-invasive BMI Technology

Non-invasive BMI technology focused on detecting and enhancing learning efficiency has begun to surface in commercial applications. For example, BrainCo's Focus headband captures brainwave signals, converting them into indices to track learners' attention in real-time. The product's accompanying app offers a 21-day training program to cultivate the habit of maintaining focus.

Although such products are still in the early stages of practical application, with effectiveness and precision requiring further enhancement, they signify the transition of BMI technology from science fiction to reality, steadily integrating into our daily lives.

In conclusion, BMI technology, especially non-invasive forms, is a testament to the progress in neuroscience and a promising tool for revolutionizing educational methods and enhancing learning efficiency. As these technologies evolve, their potential impact on education and learning processes is immense, opening new avenues for understanding and improving cognitive functions in learning environments.

3.2.3 Personalized Learning Plans: A BMI Approach

The Shift from One-Size-Fits-All Education

Traditional education often follows a standardized curriculum, failing to cater to individual students' unique needs and capabilities. Every learner's developmental stages, understanding, learning pace, style, and interests differ. Therefore, tailored learning plans are essential to unlock their full potential. Personalized learning not only boosts academic performance but also enhances motivation and engagement in students.

BMIs: Superior to AI in Personalizing Education

BMIs promise to be more powerful, precise, and effective than AI in customizing learning experiences. First, BMIs can identify students' cognitive traits. Cognitive science suggests that individual behaviors are linked to complex psychological processes regulated by internal mechanisms like the brain. By monitoring brain electrical signals during problem-solving tasks, BMIs can analyze students' performance across various subjects and tasks. This insight is invaluable for educators to understand cognitive styles, learning preferences, strengths, weaknesses, and levels of focus and interest in different subjects.

Leveraging BMIs for Personalized Teaching Plans

Such information is a treasure trove for educators, especially in crafting personalized teaching strategies. For instance, if a student shows high brain activity in math but struggles in language, educators can adapt their teaching methods to focus more on math while providing additional support for language skills.

Real-time feedback provided by BMIs can help students grasp learning materials more effectively. By monitoring brain activity, BMIs can detect attention levels, emotional states, and cognitive loads during learning. If a student's brain activity indicates distraction or anxiety, educators can intervene promptly with additional support, content adjustments, or breaks, enhancing learning efficiency and quality.

Customizing Content Based on BMI Data

Educators can tailor educational content based on BMI data analysis, determining each student's learning pace and difficulty preferences. This approach allows educators to align teaching progress with learners' competencies, optimizing learning efficiency and outcomes. Educators can also offer students materials that challenge them appropriately, avoiding undue stress or frustration.

Conclusion

BMIs radically change educational methodologies by providing a personalized learning experience that aligns with each student's unique cognitive profile. This technology not only improves academic outcomes but also nurtures a more engaging and fulfilling learning environment, catering to the diverse needs of learners in a modern educational landscape.

3.2.4 Effective Interventions for Learning Disabilities through BMI Technology

BMIs: Addressing Cognitive Impairments

BMI technology, which can enhance cognitive abilities, offers a promising solution to learning disabilities caused by cognitive impairments. This signifies a crucial application of BMI in education.

Cognitive ability encompasses various aspects, including attention, memory, executive functions, language skills, and emotional regulation. However, certain individuals face cognitive challenges due to various reasons, leading to learning disabilities like ADHD, Autism Spectrum Disorder, and others. These disabilities can impact academic performance, social skills, and overall quality of life. Here, BMIs emerge as an effective intervention tool.

Neurofeedback Training: A BMI Application

Neurofeedback training, based on BMI, involves real-time monitoring of brain activity and feeding back specific neural indicators to the individual. This self-monitoring and self-regulation process aims to improve cognitive and behavioral aspects, aiding in tackling learning disabilities.

For ADHD, characterized by inattention, impulsivity, and hyperactivity, BMI technology offers personalized neurofeedback training. By monitoring brain activity, especially in areas related to attention control, BMIs can help individuals recognize their attention patterns and provide real-time feedback to improve focus. When attention wanes, the system can alert or motivate them to refocus, potentially enhancing performance in learning, work, and daily life.

FDA Approval and Global Research

In April 2020, the US FDA officially recognized cognitive feedback training as an auxiliary treatment method, also known as cognitive therapy or digital therapy. Institutions like Beijing Normal University, Tsinghua Medical School, and East China University of Science and Technology have developed and applied EEG feedback technology in China. For example, digital cognitive therapy systems by Beijing Normal University are being used in classrooms to improve students' attention, emotional regulation, and learning abilities.

A 2021 study published in *Neuroscience Research* analyzed EEG changes in children with ADHD before and after neurofeedback treatment. The treatment involved inhibiting theta waves (4–8 Hz) and enhancing beta waves (13–20 Hz). The study found that after digital therapy, ADHD children's brainwaves began to resemble those of healthy children, with significant improvements in inattention and hyperactivity-impulsivity symptoms.

Core Principle of Digital Therapy

The essence of digital therapy for EEG lies in BMI technology, primarily using non-invasive BMIs. These interfaces can intervene in ADHD by adjusting brainwave patterns and enhancing other cognitive abilities like memory, executive functions, and emotional regulation. By monitoring and providing feedback on the activity of relevant brain regions, individuals can learn self-regulation to better meet the demands of specific tasks.

Conclusion

With its potential in neurofeedback training and digital therapy, BMI technology is revolutionizing the approach to addressing learning disabilities. It offers personalized, real-time interventions that can significantly improve cognitive functions and learning outcomes for individuals with various cognitive challenges. As BMI technology advances, its role in education is set to transform how we support and enhance learning for those with cognitive impairments.

3.2.5 Moving beyond Rote Memorization: The Role of BMIs in Education

The traditional education model, often reliant on the cumbersome rote memorization process, has been a necessary but challenging part of learning. Whether mastering basic concepts or foundational knowledge, this form of learning lays the groundwork for more advanced understanding. Like learning a language where one starts with alphabets and vocabulary, every discipline requires grasping its fundamental concepts and terminologies. However, BMI technology promises to revolutionize this traditional learning method.

Current research suggests that human memory, unlike a computer's storage system, is not localized but distributed across various brain regions. It is theoretically feasible despite the complexity of extracting, reproducing, or writing memories in the brain. The basis of all cognitive forms, including tangible and abstract memories and emotions, is neural networks. If we can replicate the intricate structure of the brain and the process of neural signal transmission, we can address the challenges of human memory storage.

In the future, BMIs could simulate scenarios that generate human memories, allowing new information, knowledge, or experiences to be directly recorded in the brain, akin to writing data on a computer's hard drive. We could also use BMIs to strengthen certain memories or overwrite unwanted ones.

The introduction of BMI technology is set to accelerate the learning process based on knowledge memorization. People won't have to spend years mastering a skill or subject; new information can be directly recorded in the brain. Essentially, this involves mimicking the brain's memory creation process and, through BMI technology, inputting the content to be memorized into our memory systems. This unique form of knowledge transfer will significantly advance fields like science, medicine, and engineering.

Consequently, the barriers to learning complex subjects will be substantially lower. In the past, mastering intricate subjects like foreign languages, medicine, physics, or engineering required extensive memorization and academic training. In the future, BMIs will make these fields more accessible, enabling anyone to quickly grasp the essence of these subjects and build memory structures as needed. In medicine, for example, doctors and medical professionals could rapidly incorporate the latest medical knowledge and techniques into their brains, bypassing lengthy medical training. Non-medical individuals could also input essential medical knowledge for self-care, elevating medical service quality, reducing diagnostic errors, and saving more lives.

BMIs will not only accelerate the rate of knowledge acquisition but also spur innovation across various domains. BMIs could be unparalleled academic research tools, allowing scientists to access cutting-edge research results directly and efficiently. With large model technologies, AI could provide precise summaries of these findings, hastening scientific progress.

In the future, knowledge will be ubiquitous, and education will become more equitable. As BMI technology evolves, it promises to reshape the learning and knowledge acquisition landscape, making education more inclusive and efficient.

3.2.6 The Most Disruptive Learning Revolution in Human History

The impact of BMI technology on education and learning, coupled with AI and Information and Communication Technology, is poised to fundamentally transform human learning. In this new era, the reliance on memory-based learning will shift from paramount to a secondary skill. The mere thought of needing information through BMI technology can prompt AI to retrieve relevant data from the vast Internet database, presenting it in our minds in the desired format—concise, detailed, or in-depth.

This paradigm shift means learning a new language will become incredibly simple, effectively eradicating language barriers. Mastery of pronunciation and reading would suffice as comprehension, vocabulary, and grammar become less critical. AI will translate foreign languages into our native tongue in real-time within our minds and even assist in speaking a new language by presenting precisely formulated sentences in our thoughts. If pronunciation poses a challenge, AI can provide phonetic transcriptions in our native language, enabling effortless cross-linguistic communication. This revolution extends beyond language learning; AI integrated with BMI and the Internet will provide real-time access to an extensive and comprehensive English vocabulary database, eliminating the need for painful memorization.

Integrating BMI technology will transform memorization-based learning and fundamentally alter the current examination system based on knowledge content. With BMIs, we can instantly access the knowledge database's standard answers and optimal solutions, rendering traditional exams meaningless. In the age of BMIs, everyone will possess interdisciplinary knowledge—anything documented in the human knowledge database will be accessible. This marks a shift from teaching and learning historical knowledge to fostering skills in researching and creating new knowledge. In the BMI era, abilities like utilizing AI, asking why, thinking critically, and innovating will become core educational competencies.

3.3 Bringing *Ready Player One* to Reality

In the Netflix TV series *The Queen's Gambit*, there's a scene where the protagonist, endowed with extraordinary talent, imagines a chessboard and plays using her mind. Similarly, in the film *Ready Player One*, the fusion of BMIs and VR devices bridges the game with the real world. Today, with technological advancements and a deeper understanding of the brain, brain-controlled games that operate purely on thought have transitioned from concept to reality.

3.3.1 Revolutionizing Traditional Gaming

In 2022, the action-packed 3A game *Elden Ring* captivated gamers worldwide. It became a cult classic, selling over 20 million copies globally and bagging numerous awards. Among the various groundbreaking gameplay methods was streamer Perri Karyal's use of a BMI device. She controlled game characters solely through brainwaves, bypassing physical controls.

However, Perri didn't imagine actions like "running forward" or "attacking." Instead, she visualized actions easily recognizable by the BMI, linking these to specific game commands. For instance, imagining pushing a heavy object away signified an attack, while visualizing pulling something toward her represented healing. These mental images triggered specific brainwave patterns detected by her BMI device. Karyal, who holds a master's degree in psychology, extensively used EEG in her research. The EEG, a simple and painless method to record brain activity, reveals how different brain regions operate.

Perri used EMOTIV's EPOC X device to recognize four actions—push, pull, lift, and drop. Despite its limitations, it was sufficient for combat and healing in the *Elden Ring*. She integrated a gyroscope and employed Python coding for more complex movements, allowing sensor coordination for freer gameplay. She's also exploring eye tracking and facial recognition for richer interaction.

In 2018, Neurable, a Boston-area startup company, released a brain-controlled VR game, *Awakening*, which was the first of its kind. It utilized a special EEG headband designed for the HTC Vive headset, tracking large-scale brain cell electrical activity. The game, set in a government lab, enables players to use telekinesis to escape, manipulating toys using thought.

In 2021, Gabe Newell, founder of Valve Corporation (creator of Steam), predicted BMIs would supersede AR/VR as gaming platforms. He urged software developers to embrace BMIs, foreseeing their dominance in entertainment. As BMI technology evolves, imaging will no longer rely on physical display techs like AR, VR, MR, and XR; these will merely be transitional. Future imaging will be based on direct brain visualization through BMIs, bringing an unprecedented immersive experience in gaming and beyond.

3.3.2 Personalized Gaming Experiences

While replacing traditional controllers like keyboards and mice is just one aspect of BMIs in gaming, the future holds much more. As BMI technology evolves, coupled with AI, it can read human emotions to enrich gameplay and enhance the depth of experience. For instance, if a player feels tense, the game can increase challenges to heighten excitement; if relaxed, it can lower difficulty to maintain comfort. This personalization deeply engages players and boosts the game's appeal.

Take *The Witcher 3*, a classic open-world game beloved for its rich narrative. Players choose their stance in dialogues with Non-Player Characters (NPCs), influencing the story's direction. However, choices are limited to developers' presets, often not reflecting players' true feelings.

In the future, BMIs will detect and reflect players' actual emotions, influencing NPC interactions and story progression, allowing a uniquely tailored experience for each player. Games could also use specific emotions as key elements in level design, linking player emotions with the storyline.

In a hypothetical *Harry Potter*-themed game, players might need to maintain calmness to master magical skills. To escape illusions, overcoming fear and harnessing positive emotions could be essential. BMIs would control and drive these emotional responses by intervening in brainwave patterns.

For developers, BMIs provide insights for creating better experiences. Based on players' emotional responses during gameplay, they can optimize content that fails to evoke intended emotions like excitement, surprise, or sadness. This optimization would be significantly more precise with BMI technology.

In essence, BMIs will make games more immersive and variable, shaping the future direction of gaming by enhancing player engagement and emotional connection to the virtual world.

3.3.3 Beyond Just Games: The Educational and Therapeutic Potential of BMI-Driven Gaming

BMI technology in gaming offers more than innovative gameplay; it has significant educational and therapeutic value. For instance, the American startup NueroPlus has developed a brain-controlled game to assist children with

ADHD. The game, controlled through touchscreens on phones or tablets, requires children to wear headgear with sensors that detect EEG signals, including signals indicative of focused attention. The game's brainwave feedback mechanism aids children in stabilizing signals for game control.

To validate its clinical efficacy, NeuroPlus collaborated with Duke University to analyze its product's effectiveness. In their study involving 60 children with ADHD, they observed enhanced attention levels in those who played the NeuroPlus game for 30 minutes thrice weekly alongside traditional rehabilitation.

Another notable example is the *Mindlight* game by the Netherlands-based Play Nice Institute, designed for children aged 8–16 to conquer anxiety disorders. The game teaches them to confront and overcome fear in a safe space and at their own pace. Wearing NeuroSky's EEG brainwave sensor, the game measures the child's relaxation and focus levels. The brightness of a magic hat in the game, worn by the character Arthur, is controlled by the player's brainwaves. The more relaxed the player, the brighter the hat shines, aiding Arthur in his quest to save his grandmother from darkness. The immersive gameplay connects the player's emotions with Arthur's, teaching them to overcome fears and anxieties through increasingly challenging tasks.

In addition, numerous brain-controlled games exist, from enhancing focus to aiding stroke patients in rehabilitation. These games represent a significant technological revolution in gaming, bringing innovative play experiences and offering groundbreaking tools and resources for education and medical fields.

3.4 BMI: The New Frontier in Military Might

BMI technology is transitioning from science fiction to reality, attracting considerable attention and investment in military applications. As nations recognize the strategic value of BMI in technological warfare, its potential in the military domain is being explored extensively.

The potential military applications of BMI are positioning it as a pivotal area in global technological competition. In the future, battlefields and warfare are expected to evolve into realms dominated by super-intelligence and advanced technology, where the outcome hinges less on traditional tactics and soldier combat skills and more on the prowess of technological innovations. The accelerated integration of BMI in military uses is set to revolutionize the nature of battlefields, making it a transformative technology in information-driven and intelligent combat scenarios.

BMIs in the military could offer groundbreaking capabilities, such as enhancing soldier training, improving communication through thought transmission, and even remotely controlling unmanned vehicles or robotic systems using neural signals. Such advancements could lead to more efficient and less risky military operations, allowing for strategic decisions to be made faster and executed more precisely.

Moreover, integrating BMI technology with AI and machine learning could lead to advanced decision-making tools, providing military personnel with augmented cognitive capabilities. This synergy could facilitate complex data analysis, enabling real-time strategic planning and situational awareness on the battlefield.

However, the military application of BMI also raises ethical and security concerns. The possibility of neural hacking, where unauthorized entities could potentially access or manipulate a soldier's neural signals, presents a significant risk. Additionally, the ethical implications of enhancing human capabilities through technology, especially in combat scenarios, are topics of ongoing debate.

In conclusion, as BMI technology continues to evolve, its role in reshaping military strategies and operations is becoming increasingly significant. With its potential to augment human capabilities and revolutionize communication and control on the battlefield, BMI stands as a critical component in the future of military technology. However, considering its ethical and security challenges, its deployment must be approached carefully.

3.4.1 BMI in Military Service

Military applications are always at the forefront of embracing innovative technologies. Since the 1960s, the US Department of DARPA has pioneered BMI research. J. C. R. Licklider, the first director of DARPA's Information Processing Techniques Office, envisioned a concept of "man-computer symbiosis." In 1974, DARPA funded a BMI research project called "Tightly Coupled Man / Machine Systems," achieving significant progress.

In the Spring of 1998, Timothy L. Thomas, a renowned American defense expert in information warfare, penned an article titled "The Brain Has No Firewall." Reflecting deeply on the '97 Joint Military Exercises, he highlighted a major vulnerability in the US military's approach to information warfare: the focus on hardware and facilities, neglecting the protection of the brain and consciousness, the very operators of these systems.

Entering the new millennium, advancements in computing power and medical research intensified DARPA's interest in BMI. Various projects like "Cognitive Augmentation" and "Human-Assisted Neural Devices" received funding, reflecting the growing focus on BMI research.

Mike Hill, a professor at the State University of New York at Albany, in his book *On Post-human War: Computing and Military Violence*, notes that post-9/11, the US national security strategy shifted, with advancements in neuroscience providing a new battleground based on human cognition. Traditional weapons like planes, missiles, rifles, and small arms are extensions of human cognitive states. BMI technology could compress the "kill chain," surpassing traditional observational and weapon-firing methods.

Fred Charles Iklé, former US Under Secretary of Defense and Director of the Arms Control and Disarmament Agency, also emphasized the future of BMI technology in his book *The Self-destruction of the Nation*, stating, "We must pay attention to the progress of brain research. Neuroscience increasingly understands the brain's functions—intelligence, will, emotions, and the mysterious 'consciousness.'"

In recent years, DARPA's substantial annual investment in BMI projects has significantly advanced its application in the military domain. In the past five years, programs like Next-Generation Nonsurgical Neurotechnology (N3), Restoring Active Memory (RAM), Bridging the Gap+ (BG+), and Neural Engineering System Design (NESD) have been launched.

The N3 program aims to develop high-performance, wearable, non-invasive neural interfaces that record and stimulate brain activity with high temporal and spatial resolution. This novel interface is expected to revolutionize the study of brain functions and disorders and design precise therapeutic interventions for neurodegenerative diseases like epilepsy, Alzheimer's, and Parkinson's. It also serves as a platform for the next generation of non-invasive BMIs, enabling healthy soldiers to interact hands-free with military systems.

The RAM project focuses on repairing neural networks damaged by traumatic brain injuries, a common issue among veterans, especially in post-war psychological interventions and treatments, but also applicable to civilians. This implantable interface, a neural prosthesis, could improve memory and help subjects recall events before their injury. Potential applications include restoring memory in those affected by injury and Alzheimer's disease and enhancing memory in healthy individuals.

The BG+ project aims to develop new methods for treating spinal cord injuries by integrating injury stabilization, regenerative treatments, and functional restoration. The team will establish two systems: an implantable and adaptive device for acute and subacute phases to reduce injury impact and a system focusing on chronic phase functional restoration, deployable anywhere in the nervous system or related end-organs to effectively "bridge" the spinal cord injury gap.

NESD aims to create a neural interface that can communicate with over a million neurons in the brain. This device will transmit "high-level signal resolution and data transmission bandwidth" between the brain and electronic devices, converting brain waves and synaptic signals into binary codes readable by computers. The project aims to facilitate near-telepathic control of electronic devices, making prosthetics as easy to control and as functional as organic limbs.

DARPA's contracts are substantial, and many contractors are large consortia. Universities and businesses often collaborate to receive funding and subcontract work. For example, the Revolutionizing Prosthetics project was led by two groups, DEKA and Johns Hopkins University Applied Physics Laboratory (JHU/APL). DEKA Research & Development Corporation (DEKA—an acronym derived from famed inventor Dean Kamen's name) worked with two universities and a private developer, while APL subcontracted to 19 primary contractors (universities and private companies), ten secondary contractors, and collaborators from six countries. DARPA also funds BMI research outside these named projects through public support and small business innovation grants.

For instance, in 2021, Brown University, with DARPA funding, developed "Neurograins" neural grain electrodes. This coordinated network of independent wireless miniaturized neural sensors, each the size of a grain of salt, was successfully used to record characteristic neural signals associated with spontaneous brain activity.

DARPA has become the largest funder with the longest funding history in the global BMI field. Their funding has consistently driven and led global BMI research, particularly in military applications, like enhancing training and performance capabilities and providing "superpowers" to healthy soldiers.

3.4.2 BMI: A Game-Changer in Military Drone and Equipment Control

The BMI is pivotal to advancing human-machine interaction. Its value is significant in military applications, particularly in unmanned equipment control.

BMI enables two-way communication between the brain and external devices, merging human and computer strengths to create unparalleled synergistic advantages. Unlike traditional human-machine interfaces like screens, text, or other forms of communication aiding in managing complex systems and information, BMI can further enhance the efficiency of human-machine interaction and collaboration.

While BMIs operate similarly to other communication methods with computers or smartphones, like voice commands, touchscreens, keyboards, or mice, they bypass the need for physical actions. Military personnel can directly control robots, drones, fighter jets, and active network defense systems with their brainwaves and thoughts. It also facilitates collaboration with computer systems in complex military tasks.

On the one hand, military personnel can control robots, drones, and fighter jets without cumbersome physical operations. This allows for safer execution of tasks in high-risk environments and quicker responses since neural mechanisms react much faster than physical movements. Remote combat control becomes a possibility.

On the other hand, BMI can also assist military personnel in collaborating with computer systems to tackle complex military tasks. This collaboration encompasses more than just information transmission; it includes intelligent analysis and decision-making. For instance, in reconnaissance missions, military personnel can rapidly analyze sensor data through BMI and contemplate the best course of action, then transmit commands to equipment and drones via BMI. Future BMI teams can leverage AI to process initial data from manned or unmanned aircraft, reducing the cognitive load on military personnel and speeding up their observe, orient, decide, act loop. This efficient collaboration mode can increase the success rate of missions and reduce reliance on personnel.

As biotechnology and information technology develop and intersect, brain-computer interaction will emerge as the most advanced form of human-machine communication. In the military field, several countries are already exploring the development of brain-controlled weapon prototypes, potentially leading to "mind-driven" intelligent operations where weapons perform tasks based on human thoughts and consciousness. Future weapons like brain-controlled fighter jets, robots, and armored vehicles may realize intuitive and intelligent operations, enabling perception-driven decisions and strikes and revolutionizing equipment control methods.

A few years ago, DARPA began researching in this direction. The agency disclosed an Avatar project in its 2013 budget report, aiming to create robot armies controlled remotely by human brains, as in the movie *Avatar*. These remotely controlled robots would perform various tasks usually carried out by human soldiers.

The US Air Force is also actively researching how BMI technology can enhance the rapid response capabilities of fighter pilots. Its Alternative Control Technology (ACT) program includes BMI research. In 2015, DARPA initiated a project to enable fighter pilots to control multiple aircraft and drones simultaneously. In 2016, Arizona State University showcased an experiment demonstrating an operator using BMI technology to control three drones simultaneously. In the video, the operator wore a cap-like device adorned with 130 colored sensors, receiving brainwaves and decoding them into commands for the drones. By 2018, DARPA's BMI project lead announced that fighter pilots could simultaneously control three different types of aircraft using BMI technology.

DARPA's goal is to elevate "brain control" to a new level through human-machine interface/systems, such as wearable devices for diagnosing and treating battlefield diseases and injuries, augmented reality programs for battlefield decision support, and exoskeleton devices to enhance the strength and endurance of military personnel. Increasing research indicates that the connection between humans and machines will be tighter on future battlefields.

Ultimately, human thoughts could be transmitted to AI software or robots via BMI technology, and information from sensors and machines could be directly relayed back to the human brain. This seamless cognitive and remote machine warfare collaboration between humans and various forms of machine soldiers is foreseeable.

As Al Emondi, a former DARPA project manager, suggested, "As we approach the future, more autonomous systems will play a larger role in military operations, and neural interface technology can help combat personnel establish more intuitive interactions with these systems."

3.4.3 BMI: Revolutionizing Military Communication through Thought

The focus and key areas of military communication have always been encryption and decryption technologies. In current military communications, these technologies have reached new heights, matching threats' increasing complexity and severity. However, the emergence of BMIs could radically transform traditional communication systems, structures, and operational methods, leading to profound changes.

Traditional military communication relies on shared and public technical knowledge for encryption and decryption. Both parties use common mathematical foundations and encryption algorithms, protecting the communication content by safeguarding the encryption key. Theoretically, any encryption algorithm can be cracked given enough time and computational resources, meaning that the security of an encryption algorithm in traditional communication is contingent on the constraints of time and computing power. However, as computational capabilities enhance, the difficulty of breaking encryption algorithms gradually decreases.

On the other hand, BMI communication upends the rules of traditional communication technologies. This technology enables communication between parties before their conscious intentions are fully formed. It reads signals from the brain, directly linking thoughts and consciousness to the communication system, thus making communication independent of traditional physical mediums or mathematical algorithms. This mode of communication increases the difficulty of intercepting or decrypting messages, as the content depends entirely on an individual's thoughts and consciousness, which are challenging to externalize or decrypt.

The disruptive nature of BMI communication lies in its elimination of intermediate steps in traditional communication; it no longer requires the transmission and storage of plain or encrypted text. This renders traditional espionage methods ineffective, as there is no communicative content to intercept or decrypt. Additionally, BMI communication reduces the effectiveness of traditional espionage methods, such as eavesdropping, interception, and decryption, because they cannot attack and interpret an individual's thoughts and consciousness.

For instance, in 2008, the US Army funded research into a concept known as "Silent Talk" or the "thought helmet," a device intended to provide soldiers on future battlefields with the capability to communicate via brainwaves. The same year, the US Army also developed a ten-year plan to use BMI technology for "multi-person collaborative decision-making systems." This initiative aimed to assess battlefield situations scientifically and threats using a group's collective wisdom and experience. Multi-person decision-making BMI systems can effectively integrate the brain activity of a group of personnel, shortening decision times and increasing accuracy.

Using BMI to integrate humans and machines effectively represents a tactical and core strategic advantage in warfare. BMI systems can facilitate "centaur warfare," leveraging the precision and reliability of autonomous systems while maintaining the robustness and flexibility of human intelligence.

3.4.4 Enhancing Cognitive Abilities of Military Personnel

In 2006, the US military extensively summarized the experiences of modern warfare in its "Joint Information Operations" doctrine, introducing the concept of three operational domains in information warfare: the physical domain, the information domain, and the cognitive domain.

The physical domain includes command and control systems and infrastructure supporting land, sea, air, and space operations, foundational in modern warfare. The information domain consists of information and data flows, crucial for communication and command in modern conflicts.

The cognitive domain, however, refers to human cognitive activities, reflecting intangible spaces of emotions, will, knowledge, and beliefs. Modern warfare, characterized by its complexity and unpredictability, demands comprehensive battlefield surveillance, quick acquisition, and accurate interpretation of situational data for prompt decision-making and action. In this context, the cognitive domain has increasingly become a critical battleground.

Drawing from experiences in Iraq and Afghanistan, the US Army experimented with the 3rd Cavalry Regiment. While patrolling with the support of CH-47 Chinook helicopters from the 82nd Combat Aviation Brigade, a foot patrol unexpectedly encountered enemy fire. Before the soldiers could report or call for help, the Chinook rapidly arrived, processed data from various sources, and launched a fierce attack while transmitting real-time situational data to the troops and command center.

This battlefield efficacy was possible due to a system developed by US scientists integrating mobile eye-tracking sensors in soldiers' glasses and sensors measuring brain waves. When a soldier's vision interacts with the battlefield environment, the system automatically identifies objects and activities relevant to the mission. As the number of signals gathered increases, the AI system comprehends the soldier's intentions, creating clear feature extraction and higher-level emotional states. Attacks were initiated by the helicopters even before the soldiers fully processed and reacted to what they saw.

Beyond accurate situational awareness, BMIs are instrumental in cognitive-based military training. The US Department of Defense is leveraging this technology to accelerate military training, as described in DARPA's Targeted Neuroplasticity Training program. Military personnel often require special skills involving rapid perception, accurate judgment, and effective planning and execution of complex actions. Traditional training for these skills is time-consuming and demands high aptitude. Therefore, the US military sees value in technologies that can reduce the time, investment, and talent needed to acquire these specialized skills. Enhancing cognitive abilities through electrical or chemical stimulation could lead to potential military applications, such as improving memory for combat tasks or a fighter pilot's ability to process vast amounts of information. Researchers at the US Air Force Research Laboratory emphasize cognitive challenges associated with high-level multi-tasking environments, propelling research into transcranial direct current stimulation (tDCS) applications in military settings.

Applications of BMI in the military can also enhance attention alertness, reduce or alleviate pain, and manage negative emotions like fear and stress. DARPA's Electrical Prescriptions (ElectRx) project aims to develop non-pharmacological treatments for pain, systemic inflammation, post-traumatic stress, severe anxiety, and other challenges by stimulating the PNS. Commanders have long contemplated the best ways to control fear on the battlefield, and BMI technology shows significant potential in improving the ability to manage emotions.

In summary, using BMI technology in the military not only enhances situational awareness and training efficiency but also offers new dimensions in managing and enhancing military personnel's cognitive and emotional capabilities.

3.4.5 The Advent of Unmanned Battlefields

BMI technology, along with advancements in AI and the IoT, is leading toward a "military singularity," indicative of unmanned battlefields. Digital twin technology plays a crucial role in this transition. Digital twins are virtual replicas of physical systems, allowing for real-time monitoring and simulation of those systems. In military applications, digital twin battlefields represent a convergence of the physical and digital worlds, where every aspect of the battlefield, from terrain to equipment, is digitally mirrored. This integration allows for enhanced situational awareness, strategic planning, and decision-making.

As BMIs evolve, they blur the distinction between humans and weapon systems, transforming them from tools to teammates. Soldiers can execute commands more precisely through direct computer connections, enhancing perception and decision-making while supervising machine operations. This could mean future wars rely less on large ground forces and more on intelligent drones, robots, and unmanned vehicles, controlled remotely through BMIs.

BMIs could also be integrated with digital twin battlefields, connecting systems for real-time monitoring, thus improving combat readiness. These digital twins have significant tactical applications, including enhanced sensor and data access through BMIs.

Furthermore, wearable devices will enable soldiers to monitor physiological states in real-time, including heart rate and oxygen levels. These devices could automatically signal for assistance, thereby reducing casualties.

The new era of warfare will demand quick integration and interpretation of vast data from human-machine networks, necessitating advancements in AI, autonomous weapons systems, and enhanced connectivity. The fusion of BMIs, digital twins, and AI will be central to realizing these new technologies in warfare.

Former US Deputy Secretary of Defense Robert Work emphasized the shift from conventional warfare to a focus on machine learning and human-machine collaboration. In future battlefields, human thoughts may directly interact with AI software or robots, with information transmitted to and from the human brain, enabling seamless collaboration between humans and machines—a revolution spurred by BMI technology.

CHAPTER 4

THE GOLD RUSH OF BMIS

4.1 The Brain-Machine Wave Arrives

Propelled by foundational technological leaps, BMI technology is transitioning from science fiction and research to practical applications, igniting a market frenzy. BMIs represent a disruptive technological advancement of this era, even more so than AI, marking a new evolutionary phase in human society.

4.1.1 The Industrial Realization of BMIs

Recent advancements in brain science, neuromorphic engineering, and AI have heightened interest in BMIs. Significant milestones include Facebook's 2019 plan to acquire BMI startup CTRL-Labs for approximately US$1 billion and Elon Musk's Neuralink unveiling groundbreaking research, pushing BMIs from labs into public view and toward industrial application.

According to IMARC Group, the global BMI market reached US$1.5 billion in 2021, with projections to hit US$3.3 billion by 2027. Guosen Securities estimates that the BMI market could range between US$70–US$200 billion between 2030 and 2040.

The US, Japan, and Europe, having established early BMI initiatives through sustained capital investment and technological accumulation, lead the global BMI domain.

The US demonstrates its superiority in the depth and breadth of BMI technology, particularly in invasive BMIs, and is a global frontrunner. Notable examples include Elon Musk's Neuralink, which received human clinical trial approval in May 2023, and the BrainGate consortium, a joint venture between Harvard Medical School and Massachusetts General Hospital, funded by billionaires Bill Gates and Jeff Bezos. Other key players include International Business Machines and undisclosed BMI research organizations.

Despite a later start than the US in BMI technology, China has made rapid progress in commercial applications and established specialized support policies for BMI-related industry chains. Numerous billion-dollar brain science and neuromorphic research projects, including BMIs, are underway. For instance, the world's first non-human primate invasive BMI experiment in Beijing succeeded in May 2023.

On October 19, 2023, a 26-year-old male underwent DBS surgery at Shanghai Mental Health Center's Minhang branch. Diagnosed with OCD and unresponsive to numerous treatments, his condition was characterized by uncontrollable, repetitive thoughts. DBS, a BMI-based treatment, involved implanting 1.27 mm diameter electrodes into targeted brain areas and using a stimulator implanted under the chest skin to emit varying signals for therapeutic purposes. The surgery, lasting three hours, was deemed a success, with post-operative CT scans confirming accurate electrode placement.

DBS for mental illness treatment offers quicker efficacy compared to pharmacological interventions. Initial effects are a noticeable one-month post-operation, with significant symptom improvement following two to three months of parameter adjustments. Post-treatment, most patients can reduce or cease antipsychotic medication usage, achieving optimal clinical outcomes.

China's practical application exploration in BMI technology has been relatively swift despite its late start. The domestic BMI industry is emerging as an investment hotspot following AI technology. Chinese tech giants like Alibaba, Huawei, and Tencent have entered the BMI field through investments and acquisitions. A surge of innovative companies in the BMI sector has also emerged.

According to Ruishou Analytics, from 2014 to August 20, 2023, China's BMI industry witnessed 170 financing events involving 60 companies, with 78 disclosed financing events totaling 5.845 billion yuan, involving 149 investment institutions. The period from 2014 to 2020 saw a steady rise, with 2021 and 2022 marking a boom, accounting for 41.1% of total events and 72.1% of the disclosed total financing amount.

BMIs, representing a convergence of multiple scientific disciplines, are not mere extensions of other technological fields but a crucial technological nexus. As an indispensable frontier technology, BMIs' potential impact spans medical, educational, and consumer sectors, promising vast market opportunities.

4.1.2 The BMI Industry Chain

In the BMI industry, the entire chain can be segmented into upstream, midstream, and downstream components, which are essential for preprocessing brain signals, signal communication, and certain aspects of signal processing.

The upstream includes brain signal acquisition equipment (such as non-invasive electrodes and invasive microelectrodes), BMI chips, processing computers / data sets and processing algorithms, system-level analysis software, and external enclosures. The midstream mainly comprises BMI product providers. The downstream encompasses various application areas such as healthcare, education and training, gaming and entertainment, smart homes, and military defense. Looking at participants in each segment of the industry chain, upstream players include chip and brain signal acquisition device manufacturers, operating system and software providers, and data analysts. Midstream is primarily dominated by BMI product providers, while downstream includes a range of application fields.

Upstream: BMI Chips and Algorithms as Core Barriers

Currently, the global development of the BMI industry chain is in its infancy, with the upstream encompassing hardware, software, and brain function research. The hardware layer includes brain signal acquisition and external control devices. Brain signal acquisition devices cover core components and devices, electrodes, BMI chips, power sources, and materials; external control devices include robotic arms, bionic hands, drones, etc. The software layer entails biosignal analysis, core algorithms, computational communication, and privacy and security. Brain function research is also a crucial aspect of software simulation and realization. As understanding of brain functions deepens and data volumes grow, future challenges will include data compression algorithms, storage technology, and high-throughput, high-speed wireless data transmission. Additionally, information authentication based on brain waves and privacy and security will be key issues addressed at the software level.

In the upstream domain, BMI chips and algorithms constitute the core barriers. In China's market, the BMI industry chain is still underdeveloped, particularly in chip development, which is weak compared to international giants like Texas Instruments and the French-Italian company STMicroelectronics.

Specifically, BMI chips encompass analog, digital, and communication functionalities. They must achieve high integration, low power consumption, and high stability, especially for invasive BMIs, posing significant design and manufacturing challenges. Currently, there are two main BMI chip solutions—generic (universal chips) and custom application-specific integrated circuit (ASIC) chips. Universal chips suit various application scenarios, while custom ASICs are designed for specific applications, offering better performance and power optimization. Enterprises and universities, including Neuralink, Brown University in the US, and Fudan University in China, have begun designing custom ASIC chips for BMIs, which are all complex in design and manufacturing.

In the signal processing stage, the mainstream feature extraction and classification recognition method is machine learning, with the industry exploring deep learning to enhance computational speed and accuracy. Each method has its strengths and applicable scenarios and cannot replace each other.

Both machine learning and deep learning require extensive brain-related data to build and train models. A major challenge for current algorithm models is insufficient underlying data collection, needing large enough data sets to enhance model precision. Increasing data collection is key to algorithmic advancement. Collaborating with grassroots medical institutions to gather patient brain data can help construct brain disease pathology databases, use incremental data for dynamic algorithm updates, and continuously improve the accuracy of brain disease algorithm models, enhancing diagnostic capabilities.

Besides BMI chips and algorithms, upstream includes brain signal acquisition devices and external devices. BMI electrodes, crucial for acquiring and capturing brain signals, are divided into invasive and non-invasive technologies. Invasive BMIs include rigid and flexible electrodes, while non-invasive BMIs include wet, dry, and semi-dry electrodes.

External devices controllable through BMIs primarily include computer systems, such as operating character input/cursor movements, and mechanical systems like robots, robotic arms, drones, etc. Currently, the Neural Engineering team at Tianjin University is one of the earliest teams in China to research BMIs. Their "Shengong-Shenji" system, the world's first artificial neural robot system applicable to full-body stroke rehabilitation, passed CFDA testing and led in main performance indicators internationally.

Midstream: BMI Product Providers

Currently, non-invasive BMIs are the main research direction, applicable in rehabilitation training, education and entertainment, smart living, manufacturing, and many other areas, with relevant domestic and international pilot or application cases. According to China Business Intelligence Network data, non-invasive BMIs account for approximately 86% of the BMI market. Invasive BMIs, with higher technological barriers and costs, mainly apply in the healthcare sector, representing about 14% of the market.

With global BMI technology progressing, the number of industry patents is rapidly increasing, and the industry is moving toward the early stages of commercialization. Over two hundred companies globally offer BMI products and services, primarily concentrated in the US and China.

China's BMI sector is in the initial stages of industry development, with most enterprises being relatively small. Regarding enterprise focus areas, only a few companies, including NeuroXess, NeuraMatrix, StairMed, Enlight Medical, and Neuracle Technology, are working on invasive BMIs among financed enterprises. In contrast, others focus on non-invasive BMI products.

Downstream: Medical Applications Remain the Mainstream Direction

BMI technology directly enables interaction between the brain and external devices, bypassing conventional brain information output pathways. Its potential in the future is significant, with BMIs expected to cover a wide range of downstream application areas, infiltrating medical, educational, entertainment, smart home, military, and other fields, becoming a key form of human-machine interaction.

However, medical applications remain the mainstream direction for BMIs and are the closest to commercialization. Data shows that in 2020, BMIs in the medical field accounted for 62% of the market. BMIs are widely used in the medical field for disease treatment and functional recovery, including rehabilitation therapy, pain management, and brain-controlled prostheses. In addition, BMI technology has been extensively applied in neuroscience, psychology, cognitive science, and other areas.

When BMIs were first proposed, they were intended for medical applications, specifically to aid disabled individuals in regaining mobility. In motor impairment diagnosis and treatment, BMIs include assistive and rehabilitative interfaces.

Assistive BMIs acquire a patient's motor intentions through BMI devices to control external devices like prostheses, exoskeletons, or wheelchairs. For example, in 2019, BrainCo's Brain Robotics, a subsidiary, could directly interface with the nerves and muscles of limb amputees, allowing users to control it with their brains. Rehabilitative BMIs, based on the plasticity of the central nervous system, provide repetitive feedback stimulation directly to the brain through BMI devices, strengthening synaptic connections between neurons for restoration. Rehabilitative BCIs are often combined with virtual reality technology to create synchronous closed-loop rehabilitation systems, generating virtual 3D spaces and providing visual feedback to users through VR devices.

In the treatment of consciousness and cognitive disorders, BMI devices can acquire and analyze the brain signals of patients in a vegetative state, assess their consciousness, diagnose consciousness disorders, and even communicate with them. This aids doctors in determining the likelihood of patient awakening and recovery, allowing targeted treatment measures.

Beyond medical applications, BMIs have also entered the commercial stage in the entertainment field. In 2020, US tech company Cognixion released a BMI-based AR headset, providing immersive experiences across various scenarios like screens, gaming, telephony, and audiovisual office work. EEGSmart developed the Udrone, a mind-controlled drone operated through a BMI. Currently, BMI gaming products mainly assess concentration in basic games, similar to the early mobile gaming industry's simple "Fishing" and "Fruit Cutting" models.

Overall, it's foreseeable that in the next three to five years, medical clinical applications will continue to dominate BMI applications. Additionally, with technological development and policy support, the BMI industry is expected to explore more use cases, with patients and consumers soon enjoying the fruits of industry advancements.

4.1.3 Perspectives on Investing in BMI

Although BMI technology is mainly in the research and development stage, the investment logic based on the BMI industry chain is relatively clear.

First, the upstream brainwave acquisition components of the BMI industry chain are the most technologically intensive, with the greatest difficulty and value.

BMI technology, categorized by the method of brainwave acquisition, can be divided into invasive and non-invasive types, each suitable for different application fields. Invasive technology involves cranial surgery followed by electrode implantation inside the brain or adherence to the cortex's surface. Therefore, it is primarily applied in the medical field, with the most likely initial applications in neurology or rehabilitation for paralysis.

Non-invasive technology, employing electrodes attached to the scalp, is simple, safe, non-invasive, and cost-effective, thus applicable in a broader range of fields, including rehabilitation training, education and entertainment, smart living, and production manufacturing.

Dividing BMIs by the direction of information flow, they can be categorized into output, input, and closed-loop feedback types. Among these, closed-loop BMIs have a broader application prospect and higher technological barriers.

Second, the midstream brainwave platforms and interface devices must wait until upstream technology enters the commercial stage before a mature supply chain can emerge.

Last, downstream application scenarios mainly involve integration with other mature industries, constituting an extension of new technology. Once upstream technology matures, practical applications will rapidly follow. For instance, BMIs applied in clinical diagnosis and neurological rehabilitation can help patients regain bodily functions, control prosthetic limbs and other assistive devices, and improve cognitive abilities. In entertainment, BMI technology can be a controller for games and VR devices, enabling players to game or interact through thoughts. In education, BMI technology can be used for cognitive and attention training.

On the one hand, looking at technological difficulty, business models and application scenarios, core barriers, and infrastructure, the invasive technology pathway has clear demand in clinical scenarios, offering actual treatment effects for various clinically related diseases. Competition in this field centers on technical thresholds, covering hard technology and high-end manufacturing. This includes electrode manufacturing, the implantation process, and the development of related chips and algorithms. Thus, for investors, focusing on relevant enterprises is crucial.

On the other hand, non-invasive technology pathways are also noteworthy. Although they have yet to reach the clinical level of invasive methods, they hold potential in specific areas, such as stroke treatment, potentially catching up with the technical features of invasive BMIs. In this field, non-invasive methods could penetrate and capture a portion of the embedded BMI market share. However, it is important to note that invasive and non-invasive technology pathways are likely complementary in the future, and investors should maintain a long-term focus on both directions.

In summary, the field of BMI technology holds extensive potential, offering innovative treatment methods in healthcare and applications in other areas like entertainment, communication, and physical enhancement. Therefore, investors should closely monitor technological developments and market changes to seize investment opportunities in the BMI domain.

4.2 "Unicorn" Companies Leading the Way

4.2.1 Neuralink: Elon Musk's BMI Dream

In BMIs, Neuralink, established in 2016 by Elon Musk, may not be the most advanced, but it certainly is the most recognized BMI company.

Pioneering Invasive BMIs

In 2016, Musk and a group of top neuroscientists founded Neuralink. As a BMI company, Neuralink is dedicated to developing implantable BMIs to enable direct communication between the human brain and computers or other devices.

We know that BMIs are divided into two modes: "invasive," requiring cranial surgery, and "non-invasive," placed on the epidermis. Invasive BMIs are more complex, offer clearer brain signal readings, and carry higher risks. Characteristically unconventional, Musk chose the "invasive" route for BMIs. His vision: enhancing human brain computation and memory capabilities and treating diseases by implanting a chip in the brain and establishing a wireless link with computers. By integrating with intelligent external limbs, we could enhance human functionalities.

In 2019, Musk and his Neuralink team released their first product, a new technique termed "brain catheterization," involving implanting electrodes in the brain to read neural signals, controllable via an iPhone.

This process involves three steps. First, a "sewing machine" and laser create holes in the skull, which is less invasive and bloodless. The neurosurgical robot "sewing machine" can safely implant six threads per minute and with minimal invasiveness. Second, a custom chip is implanted in the brain to better read and amplify signals from specific brain areas, with three in the motor area and one in the sensory area. The only external device containing a battery is installed behind the ear. Last, information is exported using wires 4–6 micrometers in diameter. These flexible wires, insulated with a material akin to glass paper and containing wires connected to tiny electrodes or sensors, cause less damage to the brain and transmit more data than materials used in other BMIs.

A year later, they developed a chip named "N1" and implanted it in a pig's cerebral cortex, successfully demonstrating real-time neuronal activity in the pig's brain. This device, named the Link v 0.9, was smaller and more efficient than the initial version, with battery life for a day like a smartwatch and wireless charging during sleep. To showcase the new device, Musk presented a group of experimental pigs, which had previously undergone surgery to implant the latest Neuralink device, at the release event. The group took about seven minutes and ten seconds. The results showed that the pigs' brain neurons reacted when

Musk touched their noses, with brain activity wirelessly transmitted to a nearby computer.

In 2021, Neuralink showcased a monkey implanted with a chip, converting its brainwaves into computer commands to play video games. By the end of 2022, Neuralink went a step further, with the monkey able to type sentences by thought. Though the monkey didn't learn to type but was controlled by the device, it demonstrated that animals could effectively complete specific tasks.

However, Musk's ambition was not satisfied with achievements in animals; he has always aimed to start human trials. Musk repeatedly mentioned "human trials" and claimed plans to implant a BMI device in his own brain. Finally, in 2023, Neuralink's human trials were approved, allowing Musk to pursue his plans.

Delayed Human Trials

Musk's Neuralink BMI human trials have been long-awaited and highly anticipated.

Since 2019, Musk has almost annually announced that Neuralink was ready for human trials. From 2019 until now, the US FDA rejected Neuralink's human trials for "brain implants to treat difficult diseases like paralysis and blindness" at least twice, citing safety risks.

In 2022, the FDA rejected Neuralink's application for human clinical trials. According to the FDA, Neuralink did not provide sufficient data to prove the device's safety and effectiveness. The agency also expressed concern that the device might cause permanent damage to patients.

As reported by Reuters, a significant concern for the FDA involved thin electrode-carrying wires potentially migrating to other areas of the brain. Migrating wires could cause inflammation, impair the function of critical brain regions, and lead to blood vessel rupture. This migration issue could also weaken the device's effectiveness, posing risks for surgical removal.

Additionally, the FDA expressed concerns about battery safety. Six current and former Neuralink employees stated that the company needed to demonstrate in animal studies that the battery was unlikely to fail. Any component failure connected to the battery current could damage brain tissue.

The FDA also questioned whether the device could be removed without damaging brain tissue. In previous reports by Neuralink, experts acknowledged the FDA's concerns but did not provide specific responses. Furthermore, the FDA worried the device might overheat and damage tissue.

Moreover, in recent years, Neuralink has been controversial for alleged animal abuse. In 2022, Neuralink faced a federal investigation in the US for purported violations of animal rights, with employees claiming unnecessary suffering and death in animal experiments due to hasty procedures.

After several months of adjustments, Neuralink claimed to have resolved these issues, alleviating concerns about implanting the device in humans. In May 2023, Neuralink officially announced FDA approval for its first human clinical trials.

On September 19, Neuralink announced on its official website the recruitment of participants for its BMI device's first human clinical trial, aimed at assessing its safety and preliminary effectiveness. This PRIME (Precision Robot-Implanted BMI) trial will use the R1 surgical robot to place the N1 implant in the brain area controlling motor intentions. N1, ultra-fine and flexible, records brain signals and wirelessly transmits them to apps decoding motor intentions.

Neuralink is seeking trial participants with paralysis due to spinal cord injuries or ALS (Lou Gehrig's disease), with no improvement at least one-year post-injury. The main trial will take about 18 months, extending to about six years, including long-term follow-up consultations.

While Neuralink has received FDA approval, the FDA remains highly concerned about safety risks during human trials. Musk's aura has made many aware of the rapidly developing BMIs, but two major hurdles are beneath the enthusiasm for technology: safety and effectiveness. The most challenging issue lies in safety, as it is not just short-term. Like other medical products, BMIs face safety reviews, including short-term safety and long-term clinical use safety issues.

As a globally renowned BMI company, Neuralink has brought the concept of BMIs to a broader audience. Despite current clinical trial obstacles, its strong technical capabilities and substantial funding remain advantageous. Of course, Neuralink's ambitions go beyond this. According to Musk's statements in recent years, Neuralink's short-term goal is to restore sight to the blind and full-body mobility to paralyzed individuals, with the ultimate aim of achieving "cyborg symbiosis" where the human brain and computers work together.

4.2.2 Synchron: First to Obtain Human Trial Approval

In the BMI sector, Synchron stands as a formidable competitor to Elon Musk's Neuralink. Established in 2012, Synchron is headquartered in the US with a research facility in Melbourne, Australia.

In April 2016, Synchron announced the acquisition of the Australian BMI company SmartStent, which held the invasive BMI technology Stentrode, jointly developed with DARPA and the University of Melbourne. Stentrode can detect brain signals in patients with paralysis and brain disorders. Additionally, the founders of SmartStent, Associate Professors Thomas Oxley and Nicholas Opie of the University of Melbourne, joined the Synchron team.

Synchron is the world's first company to receive FDA approval for human clinical trials of a permanently implanted device. Its competitive edge in obtaining this first-mover advantage lies in two main areas: product superiority and innovative implantation methods.

Regarding product superiority, Synchron developed an endovascular electrode array product called "Stentrode," designed to record brain and neural motion. Stentrode, with a diameter of 8 mm and a length of 40 mm, can carry 16 electrode sensors. Its compact size allows for easy implantation, completed in about two hours. Additionally, Stentrode is made from a flexible nickel-titanium alloy, a material widely used in implantable medical devices known for its excellent biocompatibility.

In terms of implantation method innovation, Synchron chose a different technical route than Neuralink, belonging to the semi-invasive BMI category. Synchron employs a neuro-interventional approach, inserting Stentrode into the motor cortex via the jugular vein and then integrating it with the blood vessel wall. This method avoids craniotomy, offers higher safety, and reduces infection risk, thus receiving more lenient regulatory oversight and accelerating clinical experimentation.

Synchron's clinical trials have shown promising progress. In 2019, the company conducted post-surgery experiments on four ALS patients in Australia, allowing them to send emails and tweets, access online banking, and conduct telemedicine visits. One-year data revealed no adverse reactions.

In July 2021, the FDA approved Synchron's IDE (Investigational Device Exemption) application. A year later, under FDA approval, Synchron recruited a patient at Mount Sinai Hospital in the US for clinical trials. Dr. Thomas Oxley, CEO and founder of Synchron stated, "Our technology serves millions who have lost the ability to control digital devices with their hands. We are excited to bring a scalable BCI solution to market that has the potential to transform many lives."

In 2023, Synchron revealed ongoing human clinical trials in the US and Australia to prove the safety of its BMI technology. The company is recruiting patients for an early feasibility trial to demonstrate the technology's safety. During the study, six patients are to be implanted with Synchron's endovascular stent, with about half of the enrollment process completed.

When Synchron's endovascular stent is implanted in humans, it can collect brain data and send it to external devices, enabling the control of electronic devices. Oxley explains that implanting this device in the blood vessels next to the brain's motor cortex creates a "natural highway" in the brain.

However, as Synchron's endovascular stent does not directly penetrate brain tissue, the quality of brain signals might not be perfect. But the advantage lies in relative safety during the operation. Compared to Synchron, Neuralink can obtain more accurate data through invasive BMIs but faces greater ethical challenges. Synchron's technology, both in user acceptance and clinical safety, is a noteworthy direction.

In addition to technical progress, the BMI field also shows positive momentum in funding. In December 2022, Synchron announced a funding round of US$75 million, including investments from Gates and Bezos's investment firms.

In summary, Synchron is currently the closest to commercial application in the medical field among global BMI companies, with significant potential in applications for paralyzed patients.

4.2.3 BrainCo: Leading in Product Commercialization

As a PhD student at Harvard University's Brain Science Center and an expert in neuroscience and BMIs, Han Bicheng is dedicated to the development and industrial application of non-invasive BMIs. In 2015, while pursuing his doctorate at Harvard, he founded BrainCo.

BrainCo is committed to applying foundational BMI technology across various fields, creating disruptive products, including BrainRobotics intelligent bionic hands, StarKids BMI social communication systems for autism intervention, EMG+ electromyography feedback products, Mobius intelligent bionic legs, and the FocusZen/OxyZen meditation series. Its significant lead in product commercialization and market deployment has positioned BrainCo as a leader in the non-invasive BMI sector.

Specifically, in rehabilitation, BrainCo developed the BrainRobotics intelligent bionic hand, a high-tech assistive device integrating BMI and AI algorithms. This product enables upper-limb amputees to control the bionic hand as naturally as their own, responding intuitively to arm muscle neural signals. In 2019, *Time* magazine recognized the BrainRobotics hand as one of the year's top 100 inventions. In 2020, it received the prestigious Red Dot Design Award for best design (best of the best).

In 2020, BrainCo launched the FocusZen series to make meditation and mindfulness tangible. Addressing the long-standing issue of lacking real-time feedback in meditation, BrainCo introduced a unique solution. FocusZen combines meditation with real-time brainwave monitoring, providing users immediate feedback on brainwave data. This helps beginners form habits and advance in their practice. Additionally, FocusZen has collaborated with numerous meditation masters globally to enhance user experience and offer systematic, scientific training.

BrainCo developed the Focus concentration enhancement system in education, a brain function improvement system. Combined with various software applications, it effectively enhances brain function for diverse populations. Widely used in education, sports, meditation, and autism rehabilitation, it has been adopted by the US National Weightlifting Team, Yale Summer School, and the Italian F1 Training Group. In 2018, NASA's official website featured an in-depth report on the Focus training device, and in 2020, it was included in the Chinese Ministry of Education's Future School Research and Experiment Plan as a major innovative product.

In October 2023, BrainCo launched the Easleep intelligent sleep device, focusing on contemporary sleep issues. Based on its precise EEG and physiological signal detection technology, combined with Consumer Electronics Show (CES) physical sleep aids, binaural beats, and cognitive-behavioral therapy (CBT-I), it offers a comprehensive sleep solution through AI algorithms. Easleep repeatedly topped the Tmall "Bestselling Sleep Aid" chart upon release.

On October 22, 2023, at the opening ceremony of the Fourth Asian Para Games in Hangzhou, Chinese swimmer Xu Jialing, wearing BrainCo's intelligent bionic hand, lit the torch. She controlled the bionic hand through "thought," clasping the "laurel" firmly and igniting the torch. This marked the first time a BMI-driven intelligent bionic hand lit the torch at an international sports event, exemplifying the integration of BMI technology with intelligent prosthetics in daily life.

Furthermore, on October 19, 2023, during the torch relay of the Asian Para Games in Chun'an, torchbearer Ye Jinyan wore BrainCo's intelligent bionic leg. Leveraging intelligent prosthetics and BMI technology, she smoothly completed the torch relay, demonstrating the power of technology.

These practical applications highlight the integration of BMIs and intelligent prosthetics as a critical direction for BMI application. According to 2023 data from the China Disabled Persons' Federation, there are over 85 million disabled people in China. Despite their limited visibility on streets, mainly due to physical and psychological reasons, the integration of BMIs with intelligent prosthetics can normalize bodily functions, significantly normalizing the lives of the disabled community.

4.2.4 NeuroXess: Leading Developer of Flexible Electrode Materials in China

Founded in 2021, NeuroXess Technology is a life science company focused on flexible BMIs and exploring the brain. Leveraging research from the Shanghai Institute of Microsystem and Information Technology and the Chinese Academy of Sciences, NeuroXess Technology has made a series of technological breakthroughs in developing and applying flexible materials. It has completed thousands of preclinical animal experiments and is the first company in China to have its flexible BMI technology approved for clinical ethics.

NeuroXess Technology's patents on flexible electrodes reveal its technological strengths in three main areas:

1. High Throughput. NeuroXess Technology's related technology can simultaneously record neural signals from thousands of brain neurons by adopting high-throughput design concepts and methods.

2. Flexibility. NeuroXess Technology innovatively applied traditional Chinese silk material in brain electrode implantation, developing silk protein micro-invasive implantation technology. Silk protein has natural antimicrobial properties, biodegradability, and high mechanical strength, providing natural advantages to silk-based flexible electrodes regarding biocompatibility and mechanical strength. This "Chinese-style innovation" of combining strength and flexibility has broken a key bottleneck in the clinical applications of BMIs. NeuroXess Technology's founder and CEO, Peng Lei, explains that using the controllable degradation of silk protein, electrodes are temporarily hardened for implantation and regain flexibility after the protein dissolves, eliminating the need for additional guiding devices. This innovation addresses the issue of trauma caused by neural electrode implantation. Additionally, precision location technology of neural electrodes enables automatic implantation while avoiding blood vessels, minimizing damage, and ensuring high safety levels.

3. Minimally Invasive. Minimally invasive implantation significantly reduces trauma. NeuroXess Technology hardens the flexible surface of the electrode with silk protein, making it easier to implant, and the silk protein dissolves post-implantation, restoring flexibility. Additionally, the company uses a semi-automatic surgical robot for the implantation, which performs fully sterile, high-precision, automated operations.

Currently, NeuroXess Technology targets two markets: the research market supported by the Brain Project, facilitating fundamental research tools, and the medical market for specific indications like ALS, high spinal cord injury, and blindness.

At the 2023 World AI Conference, NeuroXess Technology unveiled seven cross-disciplinary scientific achievements, including various flexible electrodes, automated research surgical robots, and high-throughput neural signal collection and analysis systems. Two scientific research subjects were NeuroXess Technology's animal employees: a two-year-old Labrador named Neo and a seven-year-old Rhesus monkey named Wukong. They underwent electrode implantation surgeries for BMIs. Neo successfully performed motion decoding while Wukong played a game using thought control. These animal experiments demonstrate that NeuroXess Technology has achieved a 100% self-researched

BMI system chain from electrode fabrication to signal collection and neural decoding.

Moreover, NeuroXess Technology has successfully conducted human clinical trials on patients with intractable temporal lobe epilepsy using flexible neural electrodes, achieving single-neuron signal recording. This success means further trials can be conducted for long-term in vivo recording with flexible neural electrodes to restore motor functions and synthesize speech for ALS patients.

As a company established less than two years ago, NeuroXess Technology's first batch of self-owned intellectual property products in flexible materials has already been successfully commercialized, and its future development is highly anticipated.

4.2.5 Blackrock Neurotech: Global Leader in Precision Electrode Products

Established in 2008 and headquartered in Salt Lake City, Utah, Blackrock Neurotech originated as Bionic Technologies, a spinoff from the University of Utah. The company is a global leader in neuroengineering, neuroprosthetics, and clinical neuroscience research tools. It boasts a team of doctoral talents from prestigious universities such as the University of Michigan, the University of Utah, and New York University. With over 20 years of specialized knowledge in BMIs, Blackrock's expertise spans materials, implantable electronics, miniaturization, systems integration, and standardization.

Despite being in operation for 15 years, Blackrock Neurotech only received its first round of funding in 2021. By selling BMI-related hardware and software to research institutions, the company became profitable by 2015.

Blackrock Neurotech offers a range of products upstream of BMI, including electrodes, data collection systems, stimulators, wireless probes, accessories, and adapters. Its Move Again BCI device was designated a Breakthrough Device by the FDA in 2021. The company aims to enable patients to use BCI devices comfortably at home.

A BMI measures signals from the human brain and controls external devices (like computers or prosthetics) through thought. Sometimes, it can also signal the brain, evoking tactile, auditory, or visual sensations. This is the basis for some scientists exploring the restoration of vision in blind individuals using BMI technology.

BCIs are categorized as medical (aiding in restoring lost functions) and non-medical (consumer) BCIs. Another classification divides BCIs into implantable and non-implantable types. So far, implantable BCIs have primarily appeared in medical applications, offering better functional performance due to higher resolution data and better information gathered from listening to single-neuron action potentials and local field potentials. These BMI systems consist of small electronic devices, hardware, and machine learning software that decode brain signals and convert them into digital commands, enabling control over external devices like computer cursors or mechanical arms.

Blackrock's BMI technology has achieved the following functions in research environments: restoring motor, sensory, and communication functions in patients with various neurological diseases and injuries (including stroke, paralysis, ALS, and limb dislocation). Blackrock is also developing and testing technologies for blindness, hearing loss, and other limiting conditions.

In the electrode domain, Blackrock Neurotech is a global leader in precision electrodes and the inventor of the renowned Utah Array. The company has developed multiple precision electrodes, including the Utah Array, Slant Array, and NeuroPort Array. The Utah Array, patented by Blackrock Neurotech, is a microelectrode array product and the industry-recognized gold standard for recording and stimulating the brain.

Utah electrodes have several advantages over other implant electrodes: high channel count, with up to 128 active electrode channels customizable to 1,024 channels; safety, with no severe adverse events related to the implant reported since its first human implantation in 2004; and long, stable lifespan, with over ten years of successful long-term recording in primates and seven years in humans. Additionally, the material properties of gallium oxide ensure stable thresholds and high charge capacity, maintaining long-term stability in electrode recording performance.

Blackrock Neurotech's electrode strengths are formidable as a supplier of foundational technology in the BMI industry. Its robust bottom-layer technology research and development capabilities are becoming the company's greatest advantage in clinical applications.

4.3 How Far Is BMI from Commercialization?

Decades ago, scientists already sensed the revolutionary impact of BMIs on both medicine and societal progress. BMIs are undeniably a formidable technological force with immense potential. So, today, amid the market frenzy over BMIs, how far are we from the practical application of BMIs? What challenges must we overcome before society fully embraces the BMI era?

4.3.1 The Commercialization Challenges of BMIs

Undoubtedly, BMIs embody our futuristic aspirations. Their potential extends far beyond medical applications.

In addition to aiding paralyzed patients to regain mobility, BMIs could be used to treat a range of conditions, including obesity, autism, depression, and schizophrenia. Shortly, BMIs might even take over the human function of memory storage.

As a communication system between the brain and the external world, BMIs could significantly enhance brain functions, offering limitless memory, accelerated computing, heightened positive sensations, improved focus, and enhanced auditory and visual perceptions. They might even enable telepathy. Taking a step further, based on the principle of BMIs, where neural impulses are networks of electrical and chemical signals, these impulses could be converted into analog and digital signals. This implies that BMIs could electronically digitize human memories and consciousness, potentially achieving digital immortality.

However, the complexity and variability of life sciences far surpass other fields, and the journey from a brilliant idea to practical realization faces greater challenges.

First, the biggest hurdle for BMI implementation is safety. During animal testing, Neuralink faced numerous allegations.

In February 2022, the Physicians Committee for Responsible Medicine announced plans to file a complaint with the US Department of Agriculture against Neuralink and the University of California-Davis. They accused them of invasive and fatal brain experiments on 23 monkeys between 2018 and 2020, violating the Federal Animal Welfare Act. In March, a nonprofit revealed that 15 of the 23 monkeys used in Neuralink's BMI experiments had died. Reports claimed that since 2018, about 1,500 animals, including over 280 sheep, pigs, and monkeys, died in Neuralink's experiments. The high animal mortality rate alarmed the FDA, leading to the rejection of Neuralink's trial application in March, with dozens of reasons cited.

Though Neuralink has received FDA approval, the FDA remains highly concerned about safety risks during human trials. Cristin Welle, a former FDA official and associate professor of neurosurgery and physiology at the University of Colorado, believes it will take at least five to ten years for Neuralink to commercialize.

More importantly, the development of BMI technology is closely linked to advancements in brain science. Despite the current hype, short-term revolutionary innovations in medical applications are unlikely, as our understanding of the brain still needs to be improved. For example, unlike the superficial motor and somatosensory cortices in mental health, the brain areas involved in emotions, memory, and cognition are more complex and less understood.

This means that while current BMI technology can address certain issues in clinical use, long-term safety remains a formidable challenge. Particularly for invasive BMIs, questions arise about potential destructive impacts on the brain from prolonged use of electronic components and irreversible damage from constant electrical stimulation of neurons. Could BMIs lead to a new form of electronic addiction? These are challenges BMI technology must confront.

Furthermore, current research on consciousness generation, memory formation methods, and cooperation mechanisms among different cortical areas must be more conclusive. These issues directly relate to whether BMIs can connect the brain to the Internet or personal servers.

Taking memory storage as an example, the physical form of memory—whether it is the structure of neural networks or the state of molecular networks—needs definition. We first need to understand and read the memory's encoding to transfer or store memories.

Additionally, while BMIs have generated market excitement, the flip side is a few global enterprises of substantial scale are facing commercialization and scalability challenges. For instance, how to reduce costs, expand production, market effectively, and maintain competitiveness. BMIs are far from being commercialized, with leading companies like Neuralink and Synchron yet to announce commercial and scalable production.

Moreover, a unified theoretical framework for BMIs or standards must be used to evaluate BMI system performance scientifically. Commercialization and regulation need precedents. With BMI technology and the market in its infancy, the industry scale remains unclear, product compliance needs to be better, and there are no laws to follow, hindering the complete commercial development of BMIs.

4.3.2 Slow Progress in the Domestic Market

Domestic enterprises focusing on BMI technology in China are mostly on the periphery, creating smart products rather than true BMI products. Additionally, these companies need help with small-scale, disorganized approaches, market speculation, and difficulties in obtaining experimental approvals.

First, the scale of enterprises is small. In December 2022, NeuroXess, an invasive BMI company backed by multi-national investment company Shanda Group and Chinese venture capital company HongShan, completed a multi-hundred-million-yuan Series A financing, one of the highest single-round financings in the industry. However, NeuroXess, established in less than two years, has a total financing scale of less than 600 million yuan and has yet to reach unicorn status. Other companies, including BrainCo, have also yet to achieve unicorn status. BrainCo is the only Chinese BMI company with over US$200 million in financing, but it took eight years to achieve unicorn status.

Second, the approaches could be more organized. For instance, Neuracle Technology, a brainwave acquisition platform with less than 1 billion yuan in total financing in five rounds, simultaneously works on non-invasive and invasive approaches in Beijing, Shanghai, and Changzhou. Currently, the domestic BMI industry is in a state of long-term loss, with high research and development costs but low revenue. Therefore, the most advanced BMI technology research is concentrated in universities and institutions, supported by national science funds, with frontline research centered in the Chinese Academy of Sciences. BMI companies play a supporting, application, and industry regulation role.

Additionally, there is significant market speculation. For example, Chinese company ENC Digital Technology Co., which gained five consecutive limit-ups, capitalized on its "cognition" name despite clarifying it does not involve

BMI business. Overall, few listed companies in China are involved in the BMI industry.

In short, most listed companies flaunting the BMI banner merely ride the trend, like the hype around AI models. This poses high investment risks for investors due to a lack of corporate integrity; conversely, it detracts from substantial foundational research. Blindly following trends and speculation adversely affects the development of national technology, particularly cutting-edge technologies like BMIs.

Last, the difficulty of experiments is a challenge. In some universities, even basic EEG tests on humans require approval and supervision from ethical committees. Without transparency in BMI experiments, no one will know what happens. If news of experiment failures or casualties leaks, BMI research will become more conservative, slowing its development. Only three companies globally have entered human clinical trials for invasive BMIs: Neuralink, Onward, and Synchron.

In China, advancing invasive BMI experiments is challenging, as patients may not accept them, and enterprises need substantial medical resources and background. Non-invasive BMI companies mostly focus on gaming, entertainment, or conceptual packaging, often promoted as consumer electronics. The true effectiveness of these products is hard to verify, and no authoritative organizations have authenticated them.

It's evident that aside from traditional ethical issues, BMIs face technological and commercialization challenges. Realizing practical BMIs may still be a long way off.

CHAPTER 5

THE GLOBAL RACE FOR
BCI DOMINANCE

5.1 BMI Becomes a Global Technological Hotspot

BMIs are entering public awareness, heralding the next wave of technological revolution. Whether in technological leadership, national security, medical innovation, or economic growth, the impact of BMIs is even more expansive than AI. Against this backdrop, this technology, deeply influencing social life, production, and national defense, has become a hot spot in global technological competition.

5.1.1 Leading the Next Technological Revolution

Competition among major powers is not limited to traditional military and economic strength but includes technological innovation. In this era of innovation, BMIs, intersecting AI, neuroscience, and engineering, represent major powers' exploration and contest for future technological direction.

On one hand, BMI research and application involve neuroscience, delving into how the human brain processes information, controls movement, and generates thought and emotion. This research not only aids our understanding of brain mechanisms but also provides new approaches to treating neurological diseases. Deep research in this field can give major powers a leading position in neuroscience, laying new foundations for medical, biological, and cognitive scientific studies.

On the other hand, BMIs are a crucial component of AI. They enable direct communication between computers and the brain, facilitating brain-controlled technology with huge potential for developing smarter, more human-centric human-machine interaction systems. Hence, investments by major powers in this field can enhance their innovative capabilities in AI, accelerate the development of autonomous technologies, and promote the application of AI.

Beyond technology, BMIs have broad application prospects in the military, medical, educational, and entertainment sectors. In other words, by gaining a leading position in BMI development and application, major powers can guide the future development of multiple industries. This will spur domestic technological innovation and industrial upgrading and gain greater international influence, attracting global partners and fostering international cooperation.

National security has become another crucial motive for BMI development, especially in the military realm. BMI technology holds extensive potential for military and intelligence applications. By integrating BMIs with military equipment, major powers can enhance soldiers' perception, reaction speed, and battlefield adaptability. In 2020, the RAND Corporation published a report titled BMIs: Preliminary Assessments of Military Applications and Significance, analyzing potential future combat applications of BMIs and potential risks and challenges. The report suggests that despite certain risks, BMIs could likely support improved human-machine collaboration in future combat.

Moreover, BMIs can enhance intelligence gathering and analysis, thus strengthening national security capabilities. In the information age, possessing advanced BMI technology can be decisive in international security competition.

In military aspects, the US has been well-prepared. The DARPA has funded multiple BMI projects, investing long-term in non-invasive and invasive BMI technologies, including functional prosthetics, memory enhancement and recovery, neural interface stability, peripheral robotic communication control, and more, covering various BMI subfields. One key objective is to enhance the capabilities of the US armed forces.

DARPA stated, "Intelligent systems will significantly affect how our forces will operate in the future. It's time to consider the application of human-machine collaboration and how to realize it." To prepare for the future world, human-machine teams represent "the coin of the realm." The US Department of Defense has invested in developing implantable neural interfaces that transfer data between the human brain and the digital world. In future battlefields, human thoughts may be directed toward AI software or robots, with information transmitted directly from sensors and machines to the human brain. Ultimately, humans and machines can seamlessly collaborate and think together cognitively.

Furthermore, the US has attempted to restrict China's BMI development. On November 19, 2018, the US Commerce Department's Bureau of Industry and Security (BIS) listed BMIs as one of the 14 "Emerging and Foundational Technologies" subject to export control. On October 26, 2021, BIS announced plans to classify BMIs as potential emerging and foundational technologies crucial to US national security, requiring appropriate export, re-export, and transfer (domestic) controls. BIS's proposed rulemaking seeks public and industry feedback on whether such technologies could provide qualitative military or intelligence advantages to the US or its adversaries. BMIs are highly valued in the US and are becoming the next main battlefield of deep integration between biotechnology and information technology.

5.1.2 The Societal Impact of BMIs

Besides military influence, BMIs impact all social generation and life aspects, further influencing a country's comprehensive strength. For leading nations today, developing and competing in BMIs is almost imperative.

In the medical realm, investments by major powers in BMI technology can lead to enhanced innovation and treatment methods. For instance, BMIs, when combined with smart prosthetics or exoskeletons, can restore autonomy to patients with limb impairments, enabling them to perform daily tasks like walking and grasping objects. This improves their quality of life and helps alleviate their mental and physical burdens. National investments in this area can drive innovation in prosthetics and exoskeleton technologies, providing more options and opportunities for those who have lost limb functions, helping this special group reintegrate into society, and fueling technological innovation and manufacturing growth.

Similarly, the potential of BMIs must be considered in treating neurological disorders. Parkinson's disease, a neurological disorder, is often accompanied by muscle stiffness, tremors, and coordination decline. BMIs can be used for DBS by implanting electrodes into the brain's deep regions to alleviate symptoms. This treatment improves patients' quality of life, eases pain, and helps them better manage their condition. Likewise, BMIs can aid in the rehabilitation of stroke patients, rebuilding damaged neural pathways through neurofeedback and rehabilitation training. These applications could reduce medical costs, ease healthcare system pressure, and enhance patients' rehabilitation success rates.

National investments in medical BMIs not only aid in improving citizens' quality of life but also position them at the forefront of international medical innovation competition. Moreover, medical innovation provides economic growth opportunities, fostering the biopharmaceutical industry. Importantly, medical applications of BMIs make a positive contribution to social welfare. By helping disabled individuals regain autonomy and easing the burden on patients and families, this technology enhances the quality of life and promotes societal inclusiveness.

Additionally, the commercial potential of BMIs is another key reason for their development. BMIs can be applied in virtual, augmented reality, gaming, education, entertainment, and other industries. By supporting the research and commercialization of BMIs, major powers can create job opportunities, spur technological industry growth, increase GDP, and achieve economic prosperity. This could also help alleviate potential economic challenges in the future.

For instance, by integrating BMIs with VR and AR technologies, people can interact directly with the digital world through their brains, creating more immersive experiences. This is applicable not only in entertainment and gaming but also in education, training, medical, and simulation training. National investments in these areas can drive the virtual and augmented reality market growth and increase the demand for technological products and services.

The education sector can also benefit from BMIs. By utilizing BMIs, educators can better understand students' cognitive processes and adjust teaching content and methods to individualize learning, improving learning efficiency. This can enhance education quality, helping students better grasp knowledge and skills. Educational innovation will further elevate a country's educational standards, equipping future workforces with more skills.

In summary, from technological leadership to national security, medical innovation, economic growth, and social impact, these factors collectively drive major powers to invest in and promote the development of BMIs. In global competition, possessing BMI technological advantages has become important for major powers to protect national interests and achieve global leadership.

5.2 Major Power Competition, Accelerating Strategic Layout

BMIs have entered an era of technological explosion, with countries worldwide vying for strategic high ground in global BMI competition.

5.2.1 The US: Early Initiatives, Rapid Development

As early as 1989, the US government introduced the Brain Science Program, declaring the last decade of the 20th century as the "Decade of the Brain." On April 2, 2013, the Obama administration announced the BRAIN Initiative (Brain Research through Advancing Innovative Neurotechnologies), aimed at exploring human brain mechanics, mapping brain activity, advancing neuroscience research, and developing new therapies for currently incurable brain diseases. The US government initially allocated over US$100 million in startup funding, which was later adjusted to plan a total investment of US$4.5 billion over the next 12 years.

Subsequently, three major federal agencies—the National Institutes of Health (NIH), the National Science Foundation (NSF), and the DARPA—initiated discussions and outlined their research focuses. NIH is committed to developing new tools and technologies for BMIs, their application in brain diseases, and the study of neuroethical issues; NSF focuses on new conceptual paradigms and designs in BMIs; DARPA emphasizes restoring neural and behavioral functions after brain trauma and applications to enhance human performance. Additionally, the FDA is responsible for policy formulation to promote BMI device marketing and improve regulatory transparency for neural medical devices; the Department of Commerce implements technology control plans to regulate BMI technologies.

Specifically, the US NIH developed the implementation plan for the BRAIN Initiative based on promoting unprecedented interdisciplinary research. In

2014, the BRAIN2025: A Scientific Vision report was published, finalizing the implementation plan with seven major goals and core principles. The report recommended that the BRAIN Initiative be implemented in two five-year phases, with the first phase focusing on technology development and the second on technology integration.

In 2019, the NIH's Advisory Committee to the Director's BRAIN Initiative Working Group reviewed the progress of the BRAIN Initiative, identified opportunities for applying new tools and valuable technology development areas, and submitted the BRAIN 2.0: From Cells to Circuits, toward Cures report, outlining eight priority areas for the BRAIN 2.0 phase, along with short and long-term development goals for each area.

NSF launched the "Understanding the Brain" initiative, investing in interdisciplinary research, technology, talent development, and infrastructure support, aiming to generate physical and conceptual tools to understand brain activity for a comprehensive understanding of thoughts, memory, and behavior in the brain. The National Science Foundation's focus on "brain-inspired" concepts and designs directly relates to BMIs, aiming to inspire novel paradigms, innovative technologies, and designs from the knowledge constructed by the BRAIN Initiative.

Over the past decade, NSF has gradually increased funding for cutting-edge BMI technologies, with 63% of funded BMI projects from 2013 to October 2022 focusing on new technology directions like cortical BMIs, ultrasonic BMIs, real-time non-invasive BMIs, wireless minimally invasive BMIs, and bidirectional BMIs.

DARPA, particularly focused on cutting-edge BMI research, has initiated over 20 programs and projects, concentrating on using BMI technology to reconstruct neural and behavioral functions and improve training to enhance human capabilities.

In 1974, DARPA launched the Closely Coupled Man-Machine Systems Program to use electroencephalography or magnetoencephalography to measure brain signals for direct communication between humans and machines and monitor neural states related to alertness, fatigue, emotions, decision-making, perception, and general cognitive abilities.

From 2006 to 2015, DARPA primarily deployed BMI development programs aimed at sensory and perceptual recovery and memory restoration: the

Revolutionizing Prosthetics project in 2006 to use brain-controlled mechanical arms to assist paralyzed patients with limb movements and provide tactile feedback; the deployment of reliable neural interface technology in 2010, allowing the semi-invasive BMI Stentrode to be tested, becoming the first BMI product approved by the FDA for clinical trials; the layout of hand somatosensory and tactile interfaces in 2014; the deployment of restorative encoding memory integration neural devices in 2009; and the layout of RAM and replaying memory activities in 2015, aiming to develop wireless implantable neural interfaces and closed-loop non-invasive BMIs to aid in forming new memories or searching existing ones.

Post-2016, DARPA has focused on intelligent, portable, high-resolution, high-bandwidth BMI technologies: deploying neural engineering system designs in 2016 to develop invasive high-resolution, high-bandwidth BMIs; initiating the N3 program in 2018 to develop a new generation of high-resolution, non-invasive, portable bidirectional BMIs; and launching the BG+ program in 2019 to develop novel intelligent and adaptive neural interfaces for spinal cord injury repair.

Additionally, the FDA focuses on promoting the development and marketing of BMI devices and enhancing regulatory transparency for neural medical devices. Through the IDE policy, the FDA temporarily exempts BMIs from Federal Food, Drug, and Cosmetic Act requirements during clinical research, allowing manufacturers to collect safety and effectiveness data more straightforwardly through clinical trials. Moreover, the FDA's Breakthrough Devices Program accelerates the development, assessment, and review process of BMI technologies, improving communication efficiency between manufacturers and the FDA, allocating resources for expedited review, and reducing the time required for new devices to enter the market.

In May 2021, the FDA established the "Guidance for Industry and Food and Drug Administration Staff: Non-clinical Testing and Clinical Considerations for Implantable BCI Devices for Patients with Paralysis or Amputation," offering recommendations for device descriptions, risk management, software, human factors, biocompatibility, etc., during the pre-submission phase for clinical IDE applications or marketing authorizations. Under these policies, BMI devices in the US have been approved for marketing.

In October 2021, the US Department of Commerce's BIS issued a pre-notification designating BMIs as potentially emerging and foundational technologies crucial to US national security, requiring appropriate export, re-export, and transfer (domestic) controls. This high-level attention to BMIs in the US signifies their emergence as the next battleground in the deep integration of biotechnology and information technology.

5.2.2 China: Elevating BMI to a National Strategy

Compared to the US, China places significant emphasis on neuroscience and brain-like research, elevating it to a national strategic level.

In 2016, China launched its Brain Project—focused on neuroscience and brain-like science research—consisting of two directions: brain science research aimed at unraveling the mysteries of the brain and conquering brain diseases and brain-like research directed at building and advancing AI technologies.

In 2017, four ministries jointly issued the Thirteenth Five-Year National Basic Research Special Plan, explicitly highlighting three core issues: brain and cognition, brain-machine intelligence, and brain health.

Furthermore, in the Fourteenth Five-Year Plan and the 2035 Long-Term Goals Outline, AI and brain science are recognized as national strategic scientific forces. The plan further underscores the need to strengthen original and leading scientific research, focusing on avant-garde technology areas. Here, brain-like computing and brain-machine integration technologies are key fields, with BMI technology crucial for the fusion of brain-machine intelligence.

Following the release of national policies for AI development, local governments have also emphasized neuroscience and brain-like science in their policies.

Shanghai was the first in the country to propose a local brain plan, initiating cross-disciplinary research in brain and brain-like sciences using computational neuroscience as a bridge. Formulated at the end of 2014 and launched in March 2015 with a preliminary basic research project, Shanghai released 22 influential global technology innovation center construction measures in May 2015, placing brain science and AI at the forefront of major foundational projects. In December 2018, the city initiated a major municipal project on basic transformation and application research in brain and brain-like intelligence, along with related special projects like the Whole Brain Neural Connectome and Cloned Monkey Model Plan.

Beijing has also increased policy support in relevant fields. In November 2018, the Beijing Municipal Science and Technology Commission issued six notifications to solicit reserve projects in six major technology fields for 2018, with cognitive and brain-like technology as the foremost area. In 2019, the Beijing Municipal Bureau of Economy and Information Technology published the Beijing Robot Industry Innovation and Development Action Plan (2019–2022), highlighting key works like robot learning, tactile feedback, augmented reality, and BMIs, promoting the development and production of multifunctional arms, exoskeleton rehabilitation robots, and intelligent nursing robots in elderly and health service sectors.

In 2021, Hangzhou's West Lake District took the lead in developing the brain-machine intelligence industry, aiming to build a national brain-machine intelligence industrial chain. The West Lake District's brain-machine intelligence project seeks to explore a new path with state-owned enterprises as the main body, deeply integrating industry, academia, and research. This initiative aims to make West Lake District a national demonstration area for school-district cooperation, achieving deep integration of industry, academia, and research and assisting outstanding companies and research teams to develop locally.

5.2.3 The European Union: The Human Brain Project's Setbacks

On October 1, 2013, the European Union launched the Human Brain Project (HBP), a flagship project of the European Commission's Future and Emerging Technologies, involving 135 partner institutions from 26 countries.

The HBP is a large-scale research project spanning ten years, based on supercomputing, with major research areas divided into three categories: Future Neuroscience, Future Medicine, and Future Computing. It encompasses 13 subprojects, including strategic data on the mouse brain, human brain, cognitive and behavioral architectures, theoretical neuroscience, neuroinformatics, brain simulation and emulation, high-performance computing platforms, medical informatics, neuromorphic computing platforms, neurorobotics platforms, simulation applications, social and ethical research, and project management of the HBP.

While the EU HBP does not explicitly mention BMIs, the HBP's projects are inseparable from the support of BMI technology and devices. Additionally, social and ethical research provides an ethical basis for future applications of BMIs. Researchers from countries like Austria and Germany within the EU have significantly contributed to BMI research.

Regrettably, the HBP faced challenges due to widespread academic skepticism and subsequent deviations from its initial objectives. However, during the implementation of the HBP, the EU accumulated important brain data and constructed a foundational infrastructure for brain science research, offering vital resources and platforms for BMI development through the results, data, and tools achieved at each stage.

In March 2022, as the HBP approached its conclusion, the HBP's Science and Infrastructure Board organized experts to draft the report The Next Decade of Digital Brain Research: A Vision for the Intersection of Future Neuroscience Technologies and Computing. This report aimed to establish a roadmap for the future development of the EU's Brain Project, identifying common goals and concepts for digital brain research in the next decade. The report highlighted that brain models and digital twins will drive future brain research. The application of these technologies is a long-term goal, requiring the development of critical technologies like high-bandwidth and stable BMIs. Furthermore, it underscored the immense technical and computational challenges in brain interaction, analysis, mechanism understanding, data interpretation, and processing modeling. Finally, ethical and societal issues drive responsible digital brain research.

5.2.4 Japan: Creating More Accurate Brain Maps

The Brain/MINDS (Brain Mapping by Integrated Neurotechnologies for Disease Studies) project in Japan was launched in 2014 to integrate neurotechnologies to create brain maps for disease research. The project focuses on three research areas: studies on the brains of common marmosets (South American monkeys), the development of brain mapping technologies, and the establishment of human brain atlases. The project involves BMI technologies, a field in which there has already been considerable news and literature from Japanese research.

The project will receive 40 billion yen in funding over the next ten years from Japan's Ministry of Education, Culture, Sports, Science and Technology and the Japan Agency for Medical Research and Development. The project's core objective is to combine neuroscience, medicine, and engineering technologies to create more precise and detailed brain maps, offering new perspectives and approaches for understanding the mechanisms and treatments of neurological diseases.

As early as the 2018 CES, Nissan showcased its latest research achievement, the "Brain-Controlled Car" (Nissan Brain-to-Vehicle). This innovation uses B2V technology, where the driver wears a device that monitors and decodes human brain waves, transmitting brain responses to the vehicle. In simpler terms, this is a BMI system for vehicle autonomous control.

On June 28, 2023, Japan's Ministry of Defense published the Defense Technology Guidelines 2023, summarizing the technological fields needed to strengthen defense capabilities. This was the first comprehensive guideline to use advanced technologies, such as BMI and shielding technologies, as part of a security policy spanning various ministries.

The Defense Technology Guidelines 2023 are based on the spirit of the National Security Strategy and other security documents revised in December 2022, advocating a mechanism across government departments by combining research and development needs based on the Ministry of Defense's views with technology scenarios held by relevant ministries. This is the first time the Ministry of Defense has specified concrete needs, aiming to reflect them in the budget preparation for the fiscal year 2024.

As an "important technology field to firmly protect Japan," the Defense Technology Guidelines 2023 lists 12 areas, including unmanned systems and cyber defense, emphasizing the need to focus on "securing future technological superiority" over the next decade. BMI technology is explicitly identified as one of the key technologies in the national security strategy.

5.2.5 South Korea: Focused on Fundamental Research

The Korea Brain Initiative (KBI) aims to foster interaction between brain science and industry. This initiative is spearheaded by three research institutions: the KBI, the Korea Institute of Science and Technology's Brain Science Institute, and the Neural Tool Development Team.

The KBI is dedicated to fundamental research to develop novel neurotechnologies applicable to both basic and clinical research. It focuses on clinical studies of neurodegenerative diseases, such as Alzheimer's disease (AD) and Parkinson's disease (PD). The development projects of the initiative include establishing multi-scale brain atlases, developing innovative neurotechnologies for brain mapping, enhancing research and development related to AI, and developing personalized medicine for neurological disorders.

In 2021, South Korean researchers published a new multifunctional BMI that simultaneously records neuronal activity and delivers liquid drugs to the implantation site. This technology used a microneedle array to collect multiple neural signals from one area, with fine metal wires transmitting these signals to an external circuit, enabling brain-controlled drug delivery.

Moreover, building on the construction of brain maps, the KBI is further intensifying its research efforts on diseases such as dementia, PD, depression, addiction, autism, and developmental brain disorders.

5.2.6 Australia: Incorporating BMI in Its Brain Mission

In 2016, supported by the Australian Academy of Science, the Australian Neuroscience Society, the Psychological Society, and the National Committee for Brain and Mind collaborated to form the Australian Brain Alliance. The Alliance aims to coordinate and promote strategic research on the Australian brain. In 2017, the Alliance proposed the establishment of the Australian Brain Project for five years with an investment of A$500 million. It outlined four challenges: optimizing and restoring healthy brain function, developing neural interfaces to record and control brain activity for functional recovery, understanding the neural basis of learning, and providing new insights for brain-inspired computing. The project aims to coordinate Australian brain researchers and scientists from other disciplines to decipher the brain's code.

Australia has been an early player in BMI technology. In 2022, a team of scientists from the University of Technology Sydney (UTS) developed a new type of carbon-based biosensor that could revolutionize brain-controlled robots and BMI technologies. This sensor is made from carbon-based epitaxial graphene, which is directly grown on silicon carbide substrates. The researchers combined the benefits of graphene (biocompatibility and conductivity) with the advantages of silicon technology, resulting in a biosensor with great elasticity and stability. Compared to current commercial electrodes, this sensor significantly reduces skin contact resistance (the electrical signal resistance between the sensor and the skin), thereby minimizing the loss of brain electrical signals during transmission. This sensor is robust and can be repeatedly used in high-salt environments.

The research disclosed this scalable new biosensor overcomes the three major challenges of biosensing technology: corrosion resistance, durability, and skin contact resistance, offering broad prospects for applications in brain-controlled robotics and BMIs.

Australia is also one of the leading countries exploring the military applications of BMI technology. Researchers from the UTS developed a non-invasive sensor that enables robot control merely through thought. In simple terms, this is remote control of robots using BMI technology. The Australian military is now using this technology, and plans are underway for its deployment.

The Australian Brain Alliance views the development of BMIs as one of the mission's objectives, proposing to develop new BMIs, stimulators, and recording devices to manufacture smarter, implantable, and wearable devices. These are aimed at treating brain diseases like Parkinson's, restoring sensory and motor functions, and are based on three principles: high-impact, interdisciplinary collaboration integrating various disciplines such as engineering, physics, computer science, and chemistry with neuroscience, psychology to form convergent science; establishing new funding frameworks that don't distinguish between medical and basic research to alter Australia's brain research landscape; and driving Australia's development through neural innovation.

To facilitate the transformation of basic science into practice, the Australian Brain Alliance also proposed establishing specialized multidisciplinary science incubators to foster connections between scientific discoveries and industry, driving innovation in new devices, diagnostic methods, and health and educational interventions, and stimulating the growth of emerging industries.

5.3 BMI Academic Competition

Academic papers are a crucial source of scientific intelligence, usually documenting foundational research achievements in various disciplines. The publication of papers related to BMI has been showing an increasing trend year by year, with various countries vying to secure a technological high ground in the academic field of BMI.

5.3.1 Distribution of BMI Research Capabilities

Based on data from BMI-related papers published between 2010 and 2021 on the Science Citation Index Expanded (SCIE), the US leads globally with 2,077 BMI-related papers published over a decade, followed by China. The number of papers published by these two countries significantly outpaces other nations, indicating that the US and China are at the forefront of theoretical research in BMIs.

Moreover, the US maintains a high average citation count per paper despite its large volume of publications. Generally, the proportion of a country's papers in the global total should roughly equal its proportion of highly cited papers. The US BMI-related papers account for 28.09% of the global total, but its share of highly cited papers reaches 42.97%—a difference of 14.88%, highlighting the academic influence of US publications. This demonstrates that the US excels in academic output in the BMI field and academic influence.

Conversely, despite ranking second in the number of papers published, China has the lowest average citation count among the top ten countries. With 19.43% of global BMI paper publications, China only contributes 13.24% of the highly cited papers. Thus, for China, the focus on BMI research should shift from quantity to enhancing its publications' quality and academic impact.

With a substantial number of BMI publications, Germany leads globally in average citations per paper, indicating a significant advantage in BMI research.

Looking at institutional publication data for BMI-related papers, only two Chinese institutions rank among the top 15 globally in publication volume, with the Chinese Academy of Sciences at number one. The US has four institutions in the top 15, the United Kingdom three, Germany two, and Austria, France, South Korea, and Canada each have one institution included.

Regarding citation metrics, although the Chinese Academy of Sciences ranks first globally in publication volume, its average citation count per paper is the lowest among the top 15 institutions at only 16 citations per paper. Tsinghua University, ranking 15th globally in publication volume, stands third in average citations per paper. The Technical University of Berlin in Germany holds the highest average citation count, with 60 citations per paper, followed by Stanford University in the US Chinese institutions, while increasing their output in the field of BMI, also need to enhance the quality and academic impact of their research.

5.3.2 Assessing the State of Brain-Machine Research through Patent Applications

Patents, as the carriers and outcomes of technological research, reflect the level and capacity of technological innovation. In the BMI field, the global application of all types of patents has been increasing annually.

Among the three types of patents—invention, utility model, and design—invention patents hold the highest value and technical content. According to the Derwent Innovations Index (DI), invention patents in the BMI field constitute 89.16% of all patents over the past decade, indicating high overall creativity and novelty. The grant rate of invention patents can indicate the quality of technological innovation in a field, and the average grant rate in the BMI field is 45.53%. Since 2016, the gap between the number of patent grants and applications has widened, largely due to the typical two-to-five-year grant cycle.

From January 1, 2010, to August 2, 2021, China led globally in the number of BMI-related patent applications, totaling 3,444, with 3,051 invention patents, constituting 88.59%—slightly below the global average (89.16%). The US applied for 1,299 patents, with an invention patent rate of 91.30%.

Looking at the geographical origin of patent technologies, Asian regions demonstrate strong R&D capabilities in the BMI field. China, South Korea, Japan, India, and Chinese Taipei rank among the top ten globally regarding patent applications. The other five countries in the top ten are Western developed nations: the US, Israel, Canada, Germany, and the Netherlands.

Regarding international patent applications, patents filed by an applicant from a country/region outside their own usually indicate higher technical content and broader market prospects. International patent applications are costly and time-consuming due to translation and other procedures, so their quality is generally higher. Therefore, the proportion of international patents is one of the indicators of patent quality. Although China far exceeds other countries in the number of patent applications, its international patent proportion is only 3.83%, significantly lower than Israel's 100% and even below India's 12.07%, a fellow developing country. South Korea's international patent proportion is also not high.

Among the top 20 patent applicants in the BMI field, 11 are from the US, with the first and second positions held by American companies. In total, seven American companies are among the global top 20. Five Chinese institutions are in the top 20: Tianjin University, Xi'an Jiaotong University, South China University of Technology, Hangzhou Dianzi University, and Beijing University of Technology. The Netherlands, Japan, Israel, and Canada have one organization in the top 20, with all but Japan being companies.

Enterprises play a direct role in transforming scientific achievements into products, and technology development should be enterprise-led. The dominance of universities in China's BMI research indicates a certain distance from the actual development and application of the technology.

CHAPTER 6

FROM MEMORY TRANSPLANTATION TO BRAIN ENHANCEMENT

6.1 Can Memory Be Transplanted?

Human learning usually requires a significant amount of time, and human intelligence varies in its strengths and weaknesses. Thus, transplanting someone else's brain memory into one's brain to avoid the arduous learning process or to have intelligence akin to Einstein's has long been tantalizing. In 1999, a Chinese high school exam posed the essay topic: "If memory could be transplanted." Thousands of students wracked their brains over this imaginative subject.

While memory transplantation was once a mere fantasy, today's advancements in BMI technology can make this a reality. But can memory truly be transplanted? And how would we go about transplanting memory?

6.1.1 The Secrets of the Brain

Before delving into the possibility of memory transplantation, let's first understand the organ that stores our memories: the brain.

Starting with the scalp, many believe that the inner layer of the scalp is the skull, but in reality, there are about 19 layers of material between the scalp and the skull. After traversing these 19 layers, we finally reach the skull.

Beneath the skull, the brain is wrapped in three layers of thin membranes. The outermost layer is the dura mater, a sturdy, waterproof membrane that closely adheres to the skull. Below the dura mater is the arachnoid mater, a space filled with elastic fibers, the only gap between the brain's exterior and the inner wall of the skull. These fibers help stabilize the brain's position, preventing it from moving around, and act as a buffer during head impacts. This area is filled with cerebrospinal fluid, maintaining buoyancy for the brain. The final layer is the pia mater, closely adhering to the brain's outer layer.

Once these outer layers are removed, we arrive at the brain, the most complex object known in the universe. Polina Anikeeva, a professor at MIT, describes the brain as "soft pudding that can be scooped with a spoon." Ben Rapoport, a neurosurgeon, offers a more scientific description: "a state between pudding and jelly."

The human brain is composed of three structures. The reptilian brain, the oldest part, includes the brainstem and cerebellum. Within the brainstem, the medulla oblongata controls involuntary activities such as heartbeat, respiration, and blood pressure. The pons handle swallowing, bladder control, facial expressions, chewing, saliva secretion, tear production, and posture maintenance. The midbrain, even more fragmented in function, involves vision, hearing, motor control, alertness, temperature control, and other tasks typically handled by other brain regions. The pons and midbrain also control autonomous eye movements.

The second brain structure includes critical components such as the amygdala, hippocampus, and thalamus. The two amygdala are responsible for anxiety, sadness, and fear responses. The hippocampus relates to memory. For instance, a rat navigating a maze will encode its layout in its hippocampus, with different parts of the hippocampus activating in response to different maze sections. However, after a year of other tasks, the rat may struggle to recall the maze path, as most content on the hippocampus' "scratchpad" is cleared to make room for new memories.

The thalamus, located in the brain's center, acts as a middleman for the sensory system, relaying information from sensory organs to the cerebral cortex for processing, except for olfaction, the only sense bypassing the thalamus. This exception explains why smelling salts can revive unconscious individuals. The olfactory bulb governs the sense of smell and is closely linked to the amygdala and hippocampus, hence its ability to evoke specific memories and emotions.

The third brain structure, the cortex, encompasses the entire top and outer part of the human brain. The cortex is divided into four lobes: frontal, parietal, temporal, and occipital. The frontal lobe governs personality and various aspects of "thinking," including reasoning, planning, and execution. The prefrontal cortex, at the frontal lobe's forefront, is where most human thinking occurs. The frontal lobe also controls body movements.

The parietal lobe, responsible for tactile control, primarily involves the "primary somatosensory cortex." The temporal lobe stores most of our memories and, located near our ears, is also home to the auditory cortex. The occipital lobe at the back of the head is almost entirely devoted to processing visual information.

Remarkably, the cerebral cortex, so vital and unique to humans, constitutes only the outer 2 mm of the brain, about the thickness of a coin, with the space below being a complex network of neural tissues.

6.1.2 How We Remember and Forget

After gaining a basic understanding of the brain's structures, we can discuss how we form memories. Memory is essential to our daily lives and defines "who we are." Without memory, humans would be trapped in a perpetual present. From an evolutionary perspective, intelligence, rooted in memory, is a core element of natural competition; the higher the efficiency and broader the range of memory, the easier it is to avoid competitive risks.

However, human memory could be better. Memory is a coin with two sides, intertwining the complex processes of remembering and forgetting. On one hand, excess traumatic or painful memories can burden life, as seen in post-traumatic stress disorder, repeatedly harming normal living. On the other hand, memory loss is a primary symptom of many diseases, with severity reaching an inability to manage daily tasks, such as AD. Memory is ever-present, and so is forgetting.

The study of memory has spanned over a century. Temporally, memory is classified into sensory, short-term, and long-term.

Sensory memory is the first type of memory to enter the brain: it is fleeting—like the touch of clothing on skin or the scent of a campfire. If these memories go unnoticed, they disappear without a trace. However, upon reflection, they enter short-term memory. We frequently use short-term memory in daily life, often without realizing it. For instance, we feel moved at the end of a story because we remember its beginning. After short-term memory, some important content is further processed and converted into long-term memory, lasting days or even years.

Memory acquisition, storage, and retrieval processes necessitate the coordination of different brain regions. Modern science links memory's physiological basis to the hippocampus and neocortex.

The most famous experiment by American psychologist Karl Lashley involved searching for traces of memory in specific areas of the rat's cerebral cortex. In 1935, he systematically destroyed specific brain regions in rats before and after maze training. Regardless of which brain region was damaged, trained rats escaped mazes faster than untrained ones. Lashley concluded that learning and memory abilities must relate to many different brain regions, not just one specific area.

A patient named Henry Molaison became a key figure in this theory. Suffering from severe epileptic seizures, Molaison agreed to experimental surgery. In 1953, a hole was drilled in his head, and the hippocampal region causing seizures was removed. The surgery largely resolved his epilepsy but left him with severe amnesia, unable to store new long-term memories. However, Molaison could remember most of the events from a few years before the surgery.

Molaison's memory issues indicated that the hippocampus is key to forming new memories, but the memories are stored elsewhere in the brain. The hippocampus, a large neural structure inside the brain between the thalamus and medial temporal lobe, consists of the hippocampus, dentate gyrus, and hippocampal gyrus. It has a layered structure, lacking climbing fibers but with many branches. Its cells are of two types: pyramidal cells and granule cells. Pyramidal cells form a layered pyramidal cell layer, with dendrites extending along the hippocampal sulcus. Granule cells are arranged in an orderly.

Over the past decades, the most widely accepted memory model in neuroscience is that short-term memories first form in the hippocampal region and then transfer to the cortex for long-term storage. In 1949, Donald Hebb published one of the most influential neuroscience theories of the last century.

Hebb proposed that two simultaneously active brain cells form the basis of long-term memory storage. For example, the concepts of the scent of a rose and its name repeatedly stimulate corresponding neurons in the brain. These stimuli alter the shape of these neurons and strengthen their connections. Thus, neurons linked to the scent of a rose are more likely to stimulate neurons corresponding to the rose's name. These memories persist because they become a unique part of the neural structure. The more frequently memories are recalled, the stronger and more lasting they become.

However, a 2018 study by MIT presented a new view: new memories form simultaneously in two brain areas. By associating genes and light-sensitive channel proteins related to memory-specific imprinted cells, researchers could precisely illuminate neurons activated during related memory events. This method accurately showcased the cells storing memories. Researchers then created a mouse line with learning cells responsive to light and subjected them to mild foot shocks in a special cage, inducing a fearful memory of the cage. The next day, the mice were returned to the cage, and the memory-storing cells were activated with a laser.

Surprisingly, hippocampal neurons associated with short-term memory responded to the laser. Unexpectedly, a group of neurons in the prefrontal cortex also reacted. These cortical cells formed memories of the foot shock almost immediately, much earlier than anticipated. Notably, researchers observed that, although these cortical neurons could be activated early by the laser, they did not spontaneously excite when the mice were returned to the shock-inducing cage. Since they stored memory but did not respond to normal recall stimuli, these cells were termed "silent engram cells" by researchers. Despite uncertainties about silent engram cells, they undoubtedly offer a promising direction for rediscovering hidden memories.

6.1.3 The Possibility of Transplanting Memories

Given the hippocampus' and neocortex's roles in memory storage and retrieval, a compelling question arises: can we copy or transplant human memories? While this concept may sound like science fiction, there have been numerous scientific inquiries into this possibility.

One of the earliest and most controversial was the work of American psychologist James McConnell with planarians in the 1960s. McConnell's experiments suggested that trained planarians could transfer learned behaviors when ground up and fed to untrained ones. However, these experiments have been met with skepticism and have yet to be reliably replicated, leaving their validity in question.

In terms of more advanced organisms, no well-documented experiments have successfully demonstrated the transfer of complex memories between individuals through biological means, such as the often-misattributed experiments involving bees or mice.

Modern research is exploring the memory frontier with a more technologically driven approach. Theodore Berger, a neuroscientist and biomedical engineer, has been at the forefront of this research. His work primarily focuses on developing BCIs that aid in memory functions. Berger's research involves understanding the encoding of memories in the hippocampus and creating devices that could potentially assist with memory impairments. However, the technology has yet to reach the stage of transferring specific memories from one individual to another or recording them digitally.

The concept of digitally recording or transplanting memories remains largely theoretical. While BCIs have shown promise in deciphering certain patterns of brain activity, the complexity of human memory and cognition presents significant challenges. Current research focuses on understanding these complexities and developing assistive technologies for memory rather than the direct transfer of memory content.

In summary, while the field of memory research and BMIs is advancing, the idea of memory transplantation remains speculative and faces numerous scientific and ethical hurdles. The technology, as of now, is primarily in the realm of understanding and assisting with memory functions rather than replicating or transferring memories in the way popular science fiction often depicts.

6.2 The Superpower of Memory Transplantation

Developing "memory chips" or memory transplantation products has begun in BCIs. Looking to the future, whether applied in medicine or to enhance human brain function, the realization of memory transplantation technology will bring revolutionary changes to human society.

6.2.1 A Surge in "Bionic Brains"

In 2016, a startup sparked interest in "bionic brains." Kernel, a microchip development company based in Silicon Valley, was founded by Bryan Johnson, who largely funds it. Johnson sold his payment company to PayPal for US$800 million in 2013 and then established the OS Fund, a venture fund with the goal of "rewriting the human operating system" for humanity's benefit. Unlike other Silicon Valley firms focused on AI, Kernel concentrates on "human intelligence."

In August 2016, Kernel announced an ambitious plan: to develop a clinically applicable brain prosthesis, referred to by some as "artificial hippocampus" or "memory chip," within the next few years to help people with memory problems restore or improve their memory. This "memory chip" would be implanted in the hippocampus of the patient's brain, stimulating specific neurons to help the brain function and convert input into long-term memory.

As early as 2009, Theodore Berger's team at the University of Southern California's Center for Neurobiological Biomedical Engineering had developed a neural chip that mimics hippocampal function, considered one of the significant experiments in the BCI field. Researchers implanted this neural chip in rats' brains, creating the first advanced brain function prosthesis. Subsequently, successful implantation in monkeys led them to believe the technology was ready for human trials and clinical device development.

If Kernel's project successfully turns basic science into a practical product, it could offer renewed hope for those struggling with long-term memory issues. AD is one such illness. Clinically, it presents as progressive memory impairment, cognitive dysfunction, and language disorders, manifesting as aphasia, apraxia, agnosia, and more, akin to a memory eraser gradually wiping away memories of patients and their families and friends. Unfortunately, there is still no definitive treatment for Alzheimer's.

Typically, AD develops gradually, with early symptoms often overlooked. Common symptoms include forgetfulness, loss of time awareness, and getting lost in familiar places. At this stage, the hippocampus, responsible for processing memory, begins to deteriorate. Also, the connection between the frontal lobe cortex and the hippocampus weakens, preventing the brain from properly processing short-term memory, while long-term memory distributed across various cortical areas remains unaffected. This makes patients unable to recall recent events but clearly remember incidents from decades ago.

As the disease progresses to the middle stage, symptoms become more apparent, like forgetfulness about recent events and names, losing at home, difficulty in communication, and behavioral changes like confusion and repetitive questioning. Eventually, the disease further develops, damaging even the most basic long-term memories. Patients become largely immobile, suffer severe memory impairment, fail to recognize their loved ones, lose self-awareness, and may even enter a vegetative state.

Unfortunately, there is still no cure for this disease. The road to developing drugs for Alzheimer's has been fraught with difficulty. According to incomplete statistics, there have been at least 154 publicly announced failures in drug development, with only five drugs approved for treating Alzheimer's.

Currently, there are no methods to halt the progression of Alzheimer's. Thankfully, scientists are unraveling the disease's fundamental mechanisms. With the aid of BCI technology, one promising approach is to help patients rebuild their short-term memory capabilities. Professor Berger, who studies "memory chips," has envisioned such a scenario. In brains damaged by Alzheimer's, stroke, or injury, the network of destroyed neurons usually prevents long-term memory formation. If memory chips can simulate the signal processing performed by these neurons when functioning normally, patients implanted with such chips could remember experiences and knowledge within a minute, ultimately restoring their ability to create long-term memories.

Berger says of Johnson, "He's not just after another US$800 million at Kernel. He believes the next great human challenge is improving our brains." Johnson's OS Fund supports more clinical trials. The routine treatment of epilepsy patients with temporary electrodes implanted in their brains is already part of their care. So far, in clinical trials, researchers have obtained hippocampal recordings during memory tests, and results show electrode stimulation can enhance patient memory capabilities.

However, many fundamental questions about the science of memory formation remain unanswered, making Kernel's founders' pursuit of developing a clinical memory device even more remarkable.

6.2.2 Sharing Your Memories with the World

If humanity truly achieves memory transplantation, its use in medicine might just be the most rudimentary application of this technology. The real transformative power of this technology lies beyond medical applications—it offers unprecedented possibilities for enhancing brain function. Imagine a day when memories can be recorded, transmitted, downloaded, and replayed in a transplanted brain. What changes would the world undergo?

Certainly, this process requires humans to create a detailed hippocampal neural map (or even an entire neural map of the cerebral cortex). This involves placing electrodes in various parts of the hippocampus to record the continuous exchange of electrical signals between different regions. Thus, we could capture the flow of information running through the hippocampus.

Next, we need to record the electrical pulses flowing through each hippocampus region, thereby recording memories. For example, learning a new word or a dance move triggers a complex series of electrical responses in the hippocampus, which scientists can record and analyze meticulously. Then, we could develop a "memory dictionary" correlating specific hippocampal electrical signals with certain memories.

The final step is transcribing this dictionary and transferring these electrical signals to another person's hippocampus using BCI technology. Successful uploading means they could use this electrical signal to recall the new word or repeat the dance move, even if they have never encountered this language or learned to dance. Moreover, if successful, scientists could gradually build a library containing various memory copies. Ultimately, constructing the "Human Memory Library" will be achieved.

Although we don't know how many years it will take to build this "Memory Library," scientists, including Nicolelis, believe this day will eventually come. We can envision what that scenario would be like; memory transplantation will become possible.

Then, simply by drilling a hole in your brain and implanting an electrode, all brainwaves and memories could be recorded and transmitted wirelessly to a supercomputer. You could activate the sharing mode if you wish to share your memories with the world. Afterward, anyone who wants to understand your memories could download them from the Internet and transfer them to their brain. Thus, this memory becomes implanted in their brain.

Just as taking photos with mobile phones has become a habit today, recording entire memories will also become our norm. By implanting barely visible nanowires into the hippocampus of the sender and receiver, related information could be wirelessly transmitted to a server and then converted into digital signals for Internet transmission. This way, you could upload your memories and emotions to the Internet instead of just pictures and videos. If you just climbed Mount Everest, completed a free solo climb, or jumped from a height of 10,000 meters, you could share this memory online to share your joy with the public.

At that time, individual memories will no longer be just a part of personal experience but will become a resource to be shared with others. This will change our perception of memory as a social, transferable asset. Memories will become a way for people to communicate and connect, fostering deeper understanding and empathy.

Nicolelis believes that all of this will one day become a reality. He once pointed out: "These eternal records will be cherished like precious jewels. The billions of equally unique souls who once lived, loved, suffered, and succeeded will also achieve immortality, not inscribed on cold and silent tombstones, but released through vivid thoughts, passionate love, and endured pain."

6.2.3 From Memory Transplantation to Customized Memory

The realization of memory transplantation will bring about dramatic changes in society.

First, the field of education will be revolutionized. We can choose the skills we need from a memory store, just like downloading apps on a smartphone. Skills such as memorizing English words, solving calculus problems, reading novels, or even consulting legal articles could be effortlessly mastered through memory uploading.

Future classrooms will no longer emphasize tasks that require rote memorization. The role of teachers will undergo a significant transformation, focusing more on nurturing students' creative thinking, critical thinking, and problem-solving abilities. Education will focus more on developing students' innovative potential, guiding them to explore unknown fields, and equipping them to handle complex challenges. Students will no longer need to memorize vast amounts of information but can concentrate on more inspiring and interesting activities, such as experiments, projects, artistic creation, and deep thinking. This will create more opportunities for individual growth and development.

If you aspire to become a professional doctor, lawyer, or scientist, traditional rote memorization will no longer be the main task. Memory transplantation technology will significantly reduce the burden of memorizing information required for these professions, freeing the brain from tedious memorization and allowing for greater engagement in more challenging and innovative tasks. Doctors can focus more on diagnosing and treating diseases, lawyers on legal interpretation and case analysis, and scientists on experimental design and research advancement. Suppose a great scientist is about to pass away. In that case, if the memory matter from his brain is transplanted into the minds of young scientists, his work can be continued by others. People can engage in more interesting and valuable activities.

Second, the economic and social structures of humanity will transform. Every technological revolution has left thousands of workers behind, and this time will be no exception. Some professions will disappear forever, and the scale of unemployment will be unimaginable.

With the ease of memory transfer, the value of a skill will decrease to some extent as people can quickly acquire the knowledge they need. However, this challenge will also create new opportunities. Professions will no longer rely solely on pure information memory but will focus more on creativity, critical thinking, and problem-solving skills. This will inspire many people to pursue more challenging and innovative work, driving society toward a more creative direction. In this transformation, the future of many traditional professions becomes unclear. The roles of lawyers, teachers, and doctors will undergo significant changes. Although they may no longer need to memorize large volumes of legal texts, textbooks, or medical knowledge, they will focus more on communication, information analysis, and providing customized services. Lawyers can focus more on legal interpretation and case strategy, teachers on cultivating students' creativity and critical thinking, and doctors on diagnosing and treating patients, offering more comprehensive medical care.

Besides changes in traditional professions, memory transplantation technology will also give rise to new career opportunities. Memory program developers will become an important profession, responsible for designing and maintaining memory transfer systems and ensuring the security and integrity of data. Memory management consultants may also emerge, helping individuals effectively manage and utilize their memory resources to improve learning efficiency and work performance. These emerging professions will become part of the future job market, attracting innovators and technology experts.

In theory, customized memory will become a reality within the next few decades. This prospect will create a new realm of experience for us, allowing us to live through memories that would otherwise be impossible to achieve, explore uncharted territories, admire magnificent landscapes we've never seen, feel major awards we've never won, and taste love we've never held. Realizing personalized memory can fill the gaps in our lives and satisfy the deepest desires of our hearts. Customized memories, different from daydreams or imaginations, are embedded in our brains, forming real and vivid "memories." These memories in our brains have the same perception and emotions as our personal experiences, as if they are a part of our lives. This prospect offers people unprecedented opportunities to expand their life experiences and emotional worlds through customized memories.

The realization of customized memory will also have profound impacts on multiple levels. It will change our perception of time and space. People can travel through time, returning to memories or envisioning future scenes, extending the boundaries of memory to a new dimension. This will change our interactions with the past and future, enhancing our perception of life. Additionally, personalized custom memory will provoke a rethinking of self-awareness and identity. Because these memories are rooted in the brain, they may profoundly impact our identity and emotional state. People will be the sum of their past experiences and the expression of the memories and experiences they choose. This will prompt us to rethink the nature of human consciousness and the self. Customized memory will also affect our social interactions and communication methods. People can share their personalized memories, allowing others to understand their emotions, values, and life experiences more deeply. This will foster deeper emotional connections and understanding while raising ethical and privacy issues that society needs to explore and resolve together.

The revolutionary power of memory transplantation will exceed our imagination and lead us into an unknown future full of wonder and exploration.

6.3 The Unknown Risks of Memory Transplantation

Regarding the realization of memory transplantation, while some fervently praise its future potential, others express deep concerns. Much like most new scientific discoveries, especially those related to human life sciences, medicine, and AI, they tend to spark controversy upon their emergence. Similarly, the development of BCI technology, potentially leading to memory customization and uploading, has also somewhat stirred apprehensions about the future.

6.3.1 The Remote Control of Life

Amid the eager praises and deep concerns for the realization of memory transplantation, it is much like most scientific breakthroughs, especially those in life sciences, medicine, and AI, which often spark controversy upon their emergence. The development of BCI technology, potentially leading to memory customization and uploading, has also stirred up apprehensions about the future.

In the American movie *Click*, the protagonist, Michael Newman, a successful architect, leads a busy life. Despite having a happy family with a beautiful and wise wife, Donna, and two lovely children, he never seems to have time to enjoy family life. Preoccupied with his career advancement, he isolates himself in the basement for work, frequently neglecting promises to his family. Michael always seeks a solution to end mundane tasks and reach desired moments at will quickly.

One day, Morty, a mysterious home store owner, gives him a universal remote control. Upon using it, Michael discovers its magical ability to control his life's timeline, an exhilarating feature that lets him skip tedious moments and go straight to the periods he desires.

However, the remote starts operating independently, rapidly fast-forwarding through his life. He misses many significant life moments and milestones: his promotion to a high position in the company, his wife leaving him for someone else, his father's death, and his son's wedding. Regretting his unintended negligence, Michael desperately rushes out of the hospital on a rainy night, catches up with his son, and urges him not to repeat his mistakes and to spend more time with family. Then Michael suddenly wakes up, realizing it was all a dream as he sleeps in a bed at the home store. He quickly returns home, expresses love to his once-disdained parents, camps with his children, and embraces his wife tightly. From then on, he changes his ways, prioritizing his family.

Michael's transformation in the movie is gradual, where the life remote control, allowing him to roam through life scenarios, plays a significant role. One scene depicts Michael missing his father's last moments and rewinding to his office. He sees his father's final visit, where, busy with work as a CEO, he barely acknowledges his father and even hurts him with his words before his father leaves with tears and endless regret.

While *Click* is an absurd, near-sci-fi story, and we can't whimsically travel through life stages in reality, the prospect of doing so is becoming increasingly feasible with the advancement of BCI and memory transplantation technologies.

Using VR and brainwave intervention technologies, we can easily immerse ourselves in real-life scenarios. Next, it's just about embedding a narrative for personal experience. If desired, one could even witness the unfolding of crucial life decisions at different stages. In the future, memory transplantation will further facilitate experiencing various life stages with ease. As Yuval Noah Harari mentions in *Homo Deus: A Brief History of Tomorrow*, if we can decipher the genetic code and understand every neuron in the brain, we can unlock all human secrets. After all, if humans lack a soul, and all thoughts, emotions, and sensations are mere biochemical algorithms, we could eventually bypass all experiences and directly stimulate specific brain regions to trigger emotions and feelings, leading to enlightenment instantly.

6.3.2 Authentic Experiences and False Memories

Using memory transplantation to experience the full spectrum of human life, even to catalyze epiphanies, sounds appealing. However, a critical question arises: Are these transplanted memories real?

What if people become so immersed in a world created by false memories that they never wish to return to reality? Could memory customization become a new form of mental drug or a means of thought control? Who has the right to access and use these memories? How can individual privacy and information security be protected?

More concerning is the prospect of unwanted memory customization and unpermitted memory implantation. What if someone implants memories from others or falsifies memories in our brains without our consent? What if these memories are painful, destructive, or even deadly?

Imagine this scenario. You are an ordinary citizen who happens to witness a murder and become the sole eyewitness. Your testimony is crucial for the accused. However, on the eve of the trial, you unwittingly become involved in an incredible incident.

Sitting at home, as usual, you turn on your computer to watch a newly released "immersive movie." Unbeknownst to you, this movie has been tampered with by hackers, who have illegally implanted a false memory segment, leading you to believe that the murder you witnessed was just a scene from a movie, a staged play in a studio. Consequently, your memory becomes confused, and you can no longer distinguish reality from fiction. When asked to testify in court, you cannot confirm the authenticity of what you saw. This confusion and anxiety could lead to the acquittal of the criminal suspect or the unjust accusation of innocent individuals.

Similarly, if it becomes possible to manufacture false memories associated with criminal acts, these fabricated memories could potentially be surreptitiously implanted into the minds of innocent individuals, causing them to believe that they had just taken someone's life and become murderers. Alternatively, if a criminal needs an alibi, they could secretly implant false memories into another person's brain, making that person believe that when the crime occurred, they were both somewhere unrelated to the crime scene.

Of course, these scenarios are extreme, but they are also highly plausible. In such a future, the foundations of human law would be shaken, rendering people's testimonies no longer reliable. Innocent individuals might be wrongfully convicted and subjected to undeserved punishment, while real criminals could escape justice. The legal system would descend into chaos, unable to distinguish between genuine criminals and innocent people implanted with false memories. This would lead to a crisis of trust, resulting in societal turmoil and unrest, with people losing faith in the credibility of memories and evidence.

Alternatively, we could prevent such situations from arising by enacting new laws: unauthorized access to one's memories would be considered a severe criminal offense. However, the issue remains that the death penalty cannot deter murder, and legal prohibitions may not completely eliminate such occurrences. Perhaps we need to seek technological advancements, such as marking false memories and enabling individuals to differentiate between reality and falsehood when necessary.

6.3.3 Advanced Memories and Basic Life

The notion of memory transplantation raises numerous profound questions and concerns, involving not only perceptions of reality but also the nature of thought, ethics, scientific principles, and technological challenges.

A key issue is the nature of thought patterns. Thought patterns are the product of complex neural connections and activities in the human brain, shaped over long evolutionary and social interactions. However, suppose advanced memories, like those of a genius akin to Einstein, can be transmitted to another brain. In that case, it implies that thought patterns can exist independently of the brain and human cognitive activity, contradicting all existing philosophical and scientific principles. Thought patterns are not a material entity; they rely on brain matter for existence. Extracting and transferring thoughts from one brain to another poses immense challenges since thoughts are intricately linked to specific physiological and neural mechanisms.

This leads to questions about the executors and recipients of memory transplantation. Who will perform such transfer operations? Will transferring advanced memories into any brain be effective? Is it universally applicable to all recipients? And what about transferring lower-level memories into the brains of enemies—how are these memories extracted from lower animals? These are the complex issues that memory transplantation must confront.

Human memories and thought patterns have evolved through long-term natural and social development, characterized by practical and social attributes. These patterns are deeply rooted in human biology, contributing to survival, reproduction, and environmental adaptation. For instance, our memory aids in remembering the location of food, avoiding danger, and acquiring social skills. These basic cognitive abilities have formed over extensive biological evolution. Human thought and memory are also profoundly influenced by social and cultural environments. Socialization acquires our values, beliefs, habits, and behavioral patterns. Through education, family, religion, culture, and social interaction, we absorb information and experiences, all part of our thinking and memory. Our thought patterns and memories embed social and cultural elements, reflecting our societal context and cultural traditions. Memory transplantation bypasses these processes and attributes, inevitably needing a solid foundation.

The challenges of memory transplantation extend further. If memories can be transplanted, will they adhere to a first-come, first-served order? Can they replace old memories? There are doubts about this. Additionally, whether new memories can overpower the brain's deep memories and higher consciousness, especially the subconscious, remains questionable. Numerous cases show that strong-willed individuals can summon their deep instincts and inner calls to resist the influence of dominated rational factors.

Memory is the discharge effect of numerous brain neural circuits, with incredibly complex mechanisms and astronomical combinations that must be understood from the perspective of the principle of large numbers in nature. Especially in the subtleties of memory, a slight deviation could lead to significant errors. Therefore, the difficulty of transplanting memory is unimaginable. Brain cells have potent self-repair capabilities; clinically, there are cases where brain neurons spontaneously reconnect to recover some brain functions after accidental injuries. It is certain that when new memories enter the brain, the original memories will not completely vanish, potentially hindering the new memories and causing them to fade gradually.

More challenging than memory transplantation is the inheritance of memory. How to pass on the memories of predecessors to the next generation will also be a fundamental transformation of humanity and human nature. In summary, memory transplantation might significantly change humanity and society. However, it cannot alter our inherent ability to digest and process this information. To achieve this, what we first need is to enhance our intelligence.

CHAPTER 7

THE FUTURE OF BRAIN NETWORKING BEYOND IMAGINATION

7.1 Taking the Brain "Online"

The Internet has shortened the distance between people, turning the world into a "global village." People from different countries, ethnicities, and cultures exchange information and collaborate across spatial boundaries via the Internet. The IoT further extends the capabilities of the Internet, enabling effective communication between people and objects and among objects themselves. However, despite years of development in the Internet and IoT, focusing mainly on increasing the capacity of the "transmission pipeline," the network has never possessed a higher-level characteristic—"intelligence."

So, is it possible for a network to have intelligence? Scientists have already given an affirmative answer to this question, and the core of enabling network intelligence lies in realizing the "Brain-Net."

7.1.1 Elon Musk's "Brain-Brain Interface"

In 2017, neuroscientist Tim Urban, the blogger of the well-known tech blog "Wait but Why," was invited by Elon Musk, founder of the neural connection company Neuralink, for an extensive visit. Urban had in-depth discussions with

Musk and most of the founding team members at Neuralink. Following the visit, Urban published a blog post summarizing his experience, quoting Musk: "I can imagine a flower, and I have an obvious picture of it in my mind. But if you want to describe it in words, you need a lot of language and text, and you can only describe a rough image. Your brain compresses many thoughts into slow data transmissions like speech or typing. This is language. Your brain runs a compression algorithm for thoughts and concepts. Moreover, you have to listen and decompress the information. There is also a lot of data loss in this process. So, when you're decompressing and trying to understand, you're also trying to rebuild someone else's state of mind to understand its origin and reorganize the various concepts in your mind that the other person is trying to convey. If both people have brain interfaces, you can communicate directly with uncompressed concepts."

Musk refers to this type of communication as "some kind of non-linguistic consent consensual conceptual telepathy."

Musk's dream is not novel. Sci-fi novels and movies like *Speaker for the Dead*, *The Demolished Man*, and *Avatar* have already depicted scenes of direct mental communication. Many other sci-fi stories with different themes also often portray language-less communication and direct reception of thoughts from others or other beings, linking them with human progress and the future of technology. These classic sci-fi works, to some extent, foreshadow the technological advancements Musk pursues, including neurotechnology, BCIs, and thought communication.

Of course, compared to science fiction, Musk's pursuit is more realistic. One of the initial intentions of founding Neuralink is to enable direct communication using "real thoughts" without language encoding.

However, Musk is not the first to propose the concept of a "brain-brain interface." As early as 1994, Nobel Prize-winning physicist Murray Gell-Mann mentioned in his book *The Quark and the Jaguar*: "For better or worse, one day people can directly connect with an advanced computer, not through spoken language or interfaces like a console, and connect with one or more other humans through that computer. Thoughts and feelings will be fully shared without the selectivity or deceit that language might bring. I'm unsure whether to suggest doing this, but it will undoubtedly create a new form of complex adaptive system, a true synthesis of many people."

7.1.2 "Mind-Reading" Achieved in Mice

With the rapid development of biotechnology and information technology, following the Internet and the IoT, the "brain-brain interface" envisioned by Elon Musk—a more advanced "Brain-Net"—is approaching reality.

To build a bridge between the brain and external devices, BCIs will be one of the most critical devices for "Brain-Net." Technically, the principle of Brain-Net is essentially the core theory of BCIs. During mental activities, the human brain generates a series of brainwave signals along with the functioning of the nervous system. Collecting these brainwaves and deciphering patterns using big data can translate these signals into machine-readable formats, enabling direct information exchange and control between the brain and the external world.

Brain-Net technology can be classified into two categories: invasive, which involves implanting a chip in the brain, and non-invasive, such as wearing helmets or hats capable of collecting brainwaves.

In terms of invasive technology, Brain-Net has already been validated in animals. In 2013, a research team led by neurobiologist Miguel Nicolelis at Duke University in North Carolina, implanted microchips in the brains of mice. Despite being thousands of miles apart during the experiment, these mice could still cooperate and solve simple intelligence test games via the implanted brain chips.

In this experiment, researchers implanted microchips in the brains of mice, allowing one "encoder" mouse to send instructions to another "decoder" mouse, even though they were separated in different cages. Initially, the encoder mouse was trained to react to light signals and obtain water by pressing a specific lever. The decoder mouse, connected to the encoder's brain but untrained on the light signals, pressed the lever correctly 70% of the time to receive rewards without its light stimulus, significantly more than accidental lever hits.

What surprised researchers more was the reciprocal nature of this communication. If the decoder mouse made a mistake, the encoder mouse sensed it and adjusted its brain function and behavior to better cooperate with the decoder mouse, guiding it to the correct choice.

Furthermore, the second part of the experiment involved two mice distinguishing between narrow and wide passages using tactile sensation. One mouse sent signals to help the other make the correct choice for a reward. This study demonstrated that the decoder mouse could form a dual identity by perceiving its own and its partner's whisker sensations, further proving the possibility of thought communication.

Miguel Nicolelis stated that this study was the first step in connecting the minds of multiple animals to form an "organic computer" or "brain network" for sharing information among a group of animals. This was the first instance of a "brain-brain interface," suggesting that one day, animals and humans might be able to read each other's thoughts.

In 2020, the team of Luo Minmin at the National Institute of Biological Sciences, Beijing / Beijing Brain Science and Brain-Inspired Research Center developed an optical brain-brain interface capable of transferring information about movement speed from one mouse to another, accurately and in real-time controlling the latter's movement speed.

In the brainstem is a nucleus called the nucleus incertus (NI), containing a type of neuron that can express neuromedin B (NMB). Luo Minmin's team found that the activity of these neurons could precisely predict and control an animal's movement speed. The researchers had two mice (one encoder, one decoder) head-fixed but free to run on treadmills and recorded calcium ion signal changes in a group of neurons in the NI of the encoder mouse. They transformed them into light pulse stimulation of different frequencies using machine learning. They then applied these light pulses to the same type of neuronal group in the decoder mouse's NI, allowing both mice's movement speeds to be highly synchronized.

Dr. Luo's team's work certainly advanced further than the earlier work of Nicolelis and others. The controlled activity of the decoder mouse was no longer a simple "either-or" task but a continuously variable quantity—movement speed. However, it's important to note that Dr. Luo's team didn't directly control the decoder mouse's activity using the encoder mouse's original brain signals. Instead, they had to convert the original brain manual signals into a sequence of light stimulation pulses to stimulate the decoder mouse.

Whether it's the experiments by Nicolelis' team or Luo's team, achieving "mind-reading" in mice has already proven the feasibility of brain-to-brain connections.

7.1.3 Further Progress with Non-invasive Brain-Nets

Based on invasive BCIs, the "Brain-Net" achieved in mice has been further advanced with non-invasive brain nets due to fewer technological and ethical barriers. The Rajesh P. N. Rao Laboratory at the University of Washington is one of the international centers for non-invasive brain-brain interface research. They have conducted a series of related studies since publishing their first paper on human brain-brain interfaces in 2013.

In one experiment, two participants were asked to complete a game using a non-invasive BCI: an "encoder" participant sees a missile or airplane on their screen and uses the brain-brain interface to control the "decoder" participant's hand to press a button and shoot down the missile.

The two participants were connected via a brain-brain interface device combining EEG and TMS. TMS is a non-invasive, painless, and nondestructive brain stimulation method that uses pulsed magnetic fields to affect cortical neurons, changing membrane potentials and generating induced currents, impacting brain metabolism and neural electrical activity, and thereby inducing physiological and biochemical responses, such as causing a simple movement.

In this process, the EEG signals of the sender were collected and trained to move a one-dimensional cursor by imagining wrist movement upon seeing a missile on the screen. For the receiver, the brain cortex area responsible for controlling the extensor muscles of the wrist (muscles that extend the wrist) was identified, and the TMS coil was placed above this cortex area to generate a magnetic pulse that caused upward hand movement, pressing the button.

During the experiment, the two participants were in separate buildings a mile apart, unable to hear or see each other. The sender imagined moving their wrist, generating EEG signals, which were wirelessly transmitted to the receiver's TMS device, controlling the coil to send corresponding magnetic pulses, causing the recipient's wrist to move and press the button. This enabled the two participants to cooperate and complete the game solely through the brain-brain interface.

Another brain-net experiment conducted by the Rao Laboratory involved three participants—two senders and one receiver—collaborating to complete a Tetris game in different rooms.

The study recruited 15 participants aged 18–35, including eight females, divided into three groups, achieving an average accuracy rate of 81% in five groups of experiments. Here, accuracy refers to the proportion of signals the operator receives that match the commands the receiver sends.

In the study, the three participants could not see each other and had no verbal communication, relying only on a BCI platform based on EEG and TMS.

In the experiment, only the receiver could see the randomly appearing shapes on the screen and the arrangement at the bottom. In contrast, the operator could not see the bottom of the screen, hence unable to judge whether the shape needed to be rotated. The two receivers could stare at different light-emitting diodes on either side of the screen, depending on whether the shape needed rotation, sending instructions to the operator. These diodes flashed at different frequencies: 17 Hz for "yes" and 15 Hz for "no."

The EEG electrodes connected to the receiver's head would then capture this decision signal (brainwave burst) and decode it, eventually transmitting the information to the third person's occipital lobe cortex through TMS. If the transmitted information was "yes," the operator would form a flash-like visual hallucination and could follow this information to execute the receiver's command and complete the game. If "no," no hallucination would occur.

After receiving data from the two receivers, the operator could decide to take action. The receivers could see whether the operator made the correct choice and send the next action in the subsequent round of communication, enabling the next round of game interaction.

Moreover, the study mentioned deliberate interference, reducing the decision accuracy of one receiver. However, the results showed that the operator could always distinguish between the "good" and "bad" receivers and make the correct decision, indicating that even in a complex "Brain-Net," the human brain still has the potential to filter effective information successfully.

The researchers stated, "A cloud-based brain-brain interface server could guide information transmission between any devices on the network and operate globally via the Internet, allowing cloud interactions between brains worldwide."

7.2 The Infinite Possibilities Unleashed by Brain-Nets

With the feasibility of brain-nets now confirmed, the next question is—what changes will occur if humans integrate their brains into the Internet and the IoT, allowing brains to harness the power of networked intelligence? What transformations will such a "Brain-Net" bring?

7.2.1 The Disappearance of Smartphones

Every new communication system in human history has invariably triggered profound social impacts. They define the characteristics of specific historical periods and lead human civilization forward.

Our ancestors led nomadic lives in ancient times, relying on body language and primitive sounds for communication. However, the advent of language changed everything, providing humans with a new way of communication and allowing the transfer of symbols and complex thoughts. This significant advancement led to the rise of villages and cities, propelling human society into a new era.

As time progressed, the emergence of written language further propelled the evolution of civilization. It allowed people to accumulate knowledge, record culture, and pass these precious heritages to future generations, providing the foundation for developing science, art, architecture, and great empires. The advent of written language bridged the distance between people and widened the pathways for knowledge dissemination, spreading cultural treasures far and wide.

The invention of the telephone, radio, and television further expanded the scope of interpersonal communication across continents. This revolutionary development enabled real-time communication, transcending national boundaries, and sharing ideas and cultures. This global interconnected communication accelerated the process of globalization, connecting every corner of the earth.

Like previous technological revolutions, the rise of the Internet represented another revolution in information transmission. Coupled with the emergence and popularization of smartphones, humanity entered the mobile Internet era.

In the mobile Internet era, owning a smartphone has become the norm. Smartphones allow people to communicate and disseminate information anytime and anywhere, expanding channels and methods for socializing, entertainment, work, and learning. People use smartphones for instant communication and information access; they also facilitate mobile payments for online shopping and offer entertainment content like music, videos, games, and social media. Even remote work and online education are made possible through smartphones.

The mobile Internet based on smartphones has connected the world, closely linking people globally and ushering human society into an unprecedented digital age. The free flow of information, cross-cultural exchanges, the rise of global commerce, and social networks have all become hallmarks of this era.

We are facing the next significant technological leap—the Brain-Net. This unprecedented concept will push human civilization into a new realm. In the Brain-Net, people will exchange languages and texts and instantly transmit sensations, emotions, memories, and thoughts. This communication will be done without external physical devices like smartphones or virtual reality equipment but directly presented in the brain through BCI technology. This vision surpasses any previous communication technology and has the potential to change our way of life completely and how we interact with others, technology, and the world. In the future, smartphones will completely disappear, with all communication and interaction occurring directly within our brains.

Imagine waking up and not needing to search for your phone or tablet because everything starts from your mind. You can check the news, review your schedule, and connect with family and friends through mental commands. Your brain will become an all-powerful device, replacing today's electronic gadgets. When you want to know the weather or explore global news, information will be directly presented in your consciousness without any intermediaries. This will bring unprecedented convenience, making our daily lives more fluid and efficient.

Indeed, Nicolelis had foreseen a day when people worldwide would not participate in social networks through keyboards but directly through their minds. People on the brain network will communicate thoughts, emotions, and ideas in real-time through "telepathy" instead of sending and receiving emails. Today's phone calls can only convey conversational information and tone. Video conferencing might be a bit better, as you can see people's body language at the other end of the camera. But Brain-Net will become the ultimate form of communication. Through Brain-Net, conversations can contain complete thought information, including nuances in emotions, tone, and implied meanings. Through the exchange of minds, one can share their deepest thoughts and feelings with others.

7.2.2 The Revolution in Information Search

An essential step in acquiring information is actively seeking or searching for it. We rely heavily on traditional search engines or receive information pushed by various Internet platforms. However, the advent of brain-nets will completely transform these traditional modes of search engines and information retrieval. Future searches will no longer depend on typing keywords or clicking links but will achieve instantaneous, intuitive search results based on brain consciousness. This unprecedented innovation will make information acquisition more efficient and personalized, marking the dawn of an era filled with limitless possibilities.

Traditional search engines play a crucial role in information retrieval, where we type keywords into search boxes to find needed information. However, this method has obvious limitations.

First, we must know what to search for and describe it in words. This can lead to inaccurate search results for complex questions or vague requirements. For instance, if you want to understand the symptoms of a medical condition but are still determining the correct medical term, the traditional search might not fulfill your needs.

Second, current search results take time to display. Search engines usually return dozens or even hundreds of links, requiring us to click and browse through pages to find the needed information. This process is time-consuming and cognitively demanding as we continuously evaluate the quality and relevance of the content. Searching in the vast expanse of the Internet is a time-intensive and complex task.

Brain-nets, however, will break through this "inefficiency" to the greatest extent. We will no longer need to rely on text-based keywords but can convey our needs directly through thought. This will make the search more intuitive and rapid. By thinking about what we want, search results will instantly appear in our brains. This eliminates language constraints, making searches more precise, as search engines can directly comprehend our intent.

Moreover, Brain-Net searches will significantly reduce the time and cognitive load of information retrieval. There's no need to click on links and browse pages; instead, we can directly access information relevant to our needs. This will make information acquisition more efficient, allowing anyone to quickly obtain the required information without spending much time and effort filtering and assessing search results. For example, if you're interested in astronomy, simply thinking "learn about black holes" will present you with the most relevant information, including articles, videos, and data, free from distractions of advertisements or irrelevant content.

Brain-net-based searches will also eliminate language and cultural barriers. Even today, language communication still needs to be more efficient in exchanging information. For instance, researchers often waste most of their time searching for literature and research directions rather than on experiments; in company meetings, much time is spent waiting for people or exchanging information, with substantial discussions only possible when everyone has the same background information. Brain-nets could compress the time spent on document searching and reading to nearly zero, enabling hundreds of individuals to collaborate efficiently on the same informational foundation.

Language and cultural differences have significantly challenged societal communication and information acquisition. Despite modern communication technologies making information transfer easier, language barriers must be addressed. Different languages and cultural systems can lead to misunderstandings, conflicts, and divisions. The emergence of brain-nets will fundamentally change this situation, as it no longer relies on verbal or written language for communication and information acquisition but instead directly transmits thoughts and emotions, greatly enhancing the efficiency of communication and information gathering.

Brain-nets will eliminate language barriers by turning thoughts and emotions into a shared experience. People will no longer need to translate or learn foreign languages; they can directly understand each other, regardless of their cultural or national background. Based on brain-nets, people can directly share their thoughts, memories, and emotions, allowing them to understand other cultures and backgrounds more deeply. This will greatly promote cross-cultural understanding on a global scale, breaking down cultural barriers and connecting people worldwide.

Brain-nets will bring an unprecedented sensory upgrade to humanity, such as directly implanting directions, satellite positioning information, surrounding landscapes, temperature and weather, market trends, or information needed for daily work tasks into the brain for instant retrieval. Information that used to take seconds or minutes to find can now be accessed in milliseconds. This boundless upgrade of superhuman abilities will see those connected to brain-nets process, store, analyze, and handle information at a rate several times higher than today's humans, with an accelerating increase.

Overall, brain-nets promise a world where our cognitive capacities are expanded beyond current limits, ushering in an era of enhanced human intellect and collaboration.

7.2.3 Direct-to-Brain Advertising

Brain-nets hold special commercial significance, especially for advertising and marketing, enabling more precise targeting of audiences. Traditional advertising typically uses visual and auditory media disseminated through TV, radio, the Internet, and other platforms. However, the rise of brain-nets, utilizing BCIs, will allow companies to collect critical marketing data, such as memory-activating data. This scenario will enable companies to gather more personalized consumer data, fundamentally altering how we interact with everyday devices.

Brain-nets will allow companies to "track a customer's journey, emotions, and preferences" at a deeper level and directly send customized ads and experiences to their brains or wearable devices, increasing sales. Brain-nets could also be used to "optimize Internet and TV ads." Brainwave data will replace cookie data as the new standard for future Internet-based advertising.

For the advertising industry, this is a profound disruption. As people become accustomed to Brain-Net advertising, ads will break free from traditional audiovisual media and no longer require user clicks or views. Advertising content will be directly implanted into people's brains, bypassing their explicit will, as they can be transmitted directly through brain interface technology.

Furthermore, Brain-Net advertising will achieve personalized and precise ad placements. By analyzing users' brain data, advertisers can better understand users' needs, interests, and emotional states. This allows them to tailor advertising messages based on specific characteristics and contexts of users. For instance, if a user feels hungry, they might see ads related to food, and in a pleasant emotional state, they might see leisure and entertainment-related ads. This will enhance ad effectiveness and user engagement.

If companies like Google decide to develop BCIs, they could detect whether you're paying attention to video ads, how you feel about them, and whether they're relevant to you personally. Companies like Apple could develop a BCI that selects music playlists based on your mood. Other companies could develop apps that use another company's BCI (similar to Google Play and third-party mobile apps) to collect your brain data.

Most major tech companies will also benefit from new forms of BCIs, such as those in the form of headphones. Other forms of BCIs will help bring the benefits of BCIs to the public in forms that people commonly wear. This is why brain data is becoming strategically significant for businesses.

Brain-Net advertising will also allow advertisers to control the presentation of ad messages more finely. They can create graded levels of impression depth based on commercial needs. This means they can choose what kind of impressions and emotional responses to create in users' brains to drive sales better. For example, a car manufacturer might implant positive emotions about its brand in users' brains, thereby increasing the likelihood of purchase.

More importantly, with BCI technology, regardless of whether users have already built cognition about certain goods or brands, their cognition can be replaced through BCI technology's reading and writing, building a new cognitive scenario and "memory" for users. This is memory replacement and memory construction technology, which will fundamentally change the mode of advertising. Future advertising will mainly involve memory construction and replacement. However, this is not good news for consumers, as we might lose the ability to make independent purchases, and our exhibited purchasing cognition might just be a result of BCI technology.

7.2.4 Impact on Relationships

In a future dominated by brain-nets, even the dynamics of romance and partnerships are subject to change. Typically, partner selection is influenced by individual aesthetic preferences shaped by cultural, social, and personal experiences. However, brain-nets could alter this, even allowing people to redefine and intervene in their aesthetic tastes, raising ethical and moral issues.

Specifically, we can directly intervene in the brain's perception and cognition processes through brain nets, altering an individual's perception and cognition of aesthetics. This means individuals could change their definition of beauty through Brain-Net technology, making it easier to find partners aligning with their newly defined aesthetic standards.

While this makes it easier for individuals to find partners that match their new aesthetic preferences, it raises questions about self-identity and authenticity. For example, if you originally preferred slim body types and desired a partner with a similar physique, but Brain-Net intervention led you to find healthier and fuller body types more attractive, this change in aesthetic perception could lead to conflicts with your body image and self-identity, as your appearance no longer aligns with your original aesthetic preferences.

Additionally, brain-nets can facilitate real-time visual replacement, allowing individuals to substitute the appearance of their partners with their ideal aesthetic standards in their minds. For instance, if you prefer slim partners but are with someone fuller, real-time replacement or "live photo editing" through BCI technology could create an illusion that matches your aesthetic cognition. This virtual reality experience in romance might be satisfying, but it could also lead to dissatisfaction and non-acceptance of the partner's real appearance. This raises issues of honesty and trust in relationships, as individuals might choose to hide their true appearance.

This disruption also sparks various ethical and moral questions. First, balancing technological intervention with individual autonomy is crucial. Should individuals have the right to change their aesthetic preferences, or should there be limitations to prevent unreasonable changes and interventions? Second, ensuring ethical and moral standards are upheld in applying BCI technology is vital to prevent misuse for manipulation and deception. Additionally, addressing romantic relationships' ethical and moral implications is necessary to ensure honest and healthy development.

The upheaval caused by BCI technology in romance and aesthetics will profoundly impact our society and culture. It will initiate discussions on autonomy, ethics, and morality while potentially altering the nature and honesty of romantic relationships. While the technology offers new possibilities, robust legal and ethical guidelines are necessary to ensure its application respects individual rights and upholds ethical principles. This field is complex and challenging, requiring thoughtful exploration and management.

7.2.5 Brain-Nets Revolutionizing Education

As a disruptive technology, brain-nets promises to revolutionize education. First and foremost, students will no longer need to memorize vast amounts of information, as they can access needed knowledge directly in their brains. This liberation of time and cognitive resources allows students to focus more on understanding, analyzing, and applying knowledge rather than merely memorizing and repeating it. BCI technology will transform knowledge acquisition, enabling the direct writing of new knowledge into the brain and bypassing traditional learning processes. This paves the way for rapid learning and mastery of skills.

The advent of brain-nets will fundamentally change the nature of education, making it more personalized and widespread. This transformation will profoundly impact the global education system, revolutionizing aspects from accessibility and language barriers to knowledge acquisition.

On the one hand, Brain-Net technology will facilitate more personalized education. Traditional education often employs standardized teaching methods, overlooking each student's unique needs and learning pace. Brain-Net technology empowers students with greater autonomy, allowing them to create personalized learning plans based on their interests, needs, and learning styles. Students can directly access educational materials suitable for their level and interests, free from the constraints of fixed curricula. This enhances learning efficiency and quality, as students are more likely to stay engaged and actively participate in learning, thereby better mastering knowledge and skills.

On the other hand, Brain-Net technology will make education more widespread. Education access will significantly increase, especially for people in remote or resource-poor areas. Traditional education relies on classroom setups and geographical locations, but Brain-Net technology eliminates these limitations. Students can access a wealth of educational resources via brain-nets, regardless of location. This eradicates geographical and economic barriers, allowing more people access to quality education. Students no longer need to relocate or travel to distant places for education; they can easily acquire the knowledge they need from their homes or communities.

Moreover, Brain-Net technology will break down language barriers. Education will no longer be limited to specific languages or cultures, as Brain-Net technology can directly transmit knowledge and information. Students can receive information through thought and perception, independent of specific language skills. This will make education more inclusive, as students from various backgrounds and native languages can equally access education. Additionally, Brain-Net technology will foster cross-cultural communication and understanding, as students can more easily access knowledge and perspectives from different cultural backgrounds.

When education shifts from focusing on imparting information, a question arises: Do we still need education? And what kind of education do we need? This question is relatively easy to answer. As the technological era progresses and new technologies emerge, education faces increasingly severe challenges.

AI has already demonstrated formidable learning capabilities. In this world, if it comes to rote learning, no one can surpass ChatGPT. When we ask ChatGPT a question from a regular exam, it finds the correct logic and lists every step accurately, albeit sometimes making calculation mistakes. However, adding more computing capabilities to it solves this issue. ChatGPT solves problems and absorbs a vast amount of text, including all textbooks and various problem-solving methods. ChatGPT can absorb and remember more text than humans. Moreover, ChatGPT can generate eloquent and beautifully written texts with just a slight prompt. It is now used for writing love letters, poetry, and academic papers.

The disruption brought by AI is already astounding, and BCIs will only intensify this. When knowledge acquisition becomes effortless, our challenge lies in how to use this knowledge innovatively.

In the future of education, students will need to develop more critical thinking, problem-solving, and creativity, as these skills are crucial in applying knowledge. Educational institutions and educators must rethink educational goals and methods to ensure students can successfully apply knowledge in a knowledge-rich environment, solve real-world problems, and drive societal innovation.

Furthermore, fostering innovative thinking will require an emphasis on interdisciplinary learning and collaboration. In the Brain-Net era, knowledge will no longer be confined to specific fields or disciplines, so students must possess interdisciplinary abilities to integrate and apply knowledge from different areas. Additionally, students must work together and communicate to solve complex problems as knowledge acquisition becomes so easy. Competitiveness will increasingly depend on how well one collaborates and innovates with others.

7.2.6 Immerse in the World of Entertainment

Brain-nets are set to impact the billion-dollar entertainment industry significantly. Looking back to the 1920s, sound and lighting technology advancements revolutionized entertainment, transitioning movies from silent to "talkies." This fusion of image and sound remained largely unchanged throughout the 20th century. However, a future revolution in entertainment might integrate all human senses into films and shows, including smell, taste, touch, hearing, vision, and a full range of emotions.

Brain-nets promises to process all sensations and emotions flowing through the human brain, fully immersing viewers in films and shows. Viewers watching romantic or action-thriller movies could deeply experience everything in the storyline, as if they were truly in that world, feeling every sensation and emotion of the actors. For instance, while enjoying a romantic movie or action thriller, our senses would be completely immersed in the storyline, as though we are physically present, experiencing all the sensations and emotions of the actors, creating a deeper emotional connection with the characters.

This transformative change will bring unprecedented opportunities and challenges to the entertainment industry. Producing and presenting a full-sensory entertainment experience will require significant technical and creative investment. Film production, game development, and virtual reality will see revolutionary innovations to meet audiences' demand for full-sensory experiences. In film production, directors and screenwriters will no longer be limited to visual and auditory elements; they can create more comprehensive and captivating storylines. Movies will transform from passive viewing experiences to deeply interactive full-sensory experiences. In game development, games will become more realistic and immersive. Players will feel everything in the game, from the characters' emotions to the game world's ambiance. This will drive game developers to continually enhance game engines and technology for higher levels of immersion. Brain-Net technology will make virtual reality experiences more vivid and real. Users can immerse themselves in virtual worlds and feel everything within them.

Brain-Net technology will also change the business model of the entertainment industry. Audiences may no longer need to visit cinemas or purchase physical media; they can experience full-sensory entertainment at home or anywhere through BCI technology. This will profoundly impact traditional entertainment distribution methods, requiring industry players to rethink how to adapt to this change. Entertainment companies and platforms may need to shift to subscription models or virtual reality experiences to meet new audience demands.

The impact of BCI technology in entertainment will fundamentally abandon the current metaverse, making entertainment no longer reliant on complex external devices but directly realized through brain consciousness. This means that in the era of BCI technology, current modes of entertainment, social interaction, and more will face significant challenges.

7.2.7 Demonstrating Power in the Military Field

Brain nets hold significant and powerful applications in the military sector. They could give rise to brain-controlled and mind-controlling weapon systems, akin to the US military's concept of creating Avatar-style remote human brain control systems, aiming to achieve zero casualties in combat.

Brain-controlled weapons, as the name implies, are controlled by the brain. During combat, soldiers don't need to be on the battlefield but can remotely control "proxy warriors" directly through their brains from a rear position. In 2013 and 2014, the US Department of Defense disclosed several research projects related to BCI technology, such as Avatar and Machine Legions, turning the science fiction of brain-thought-controlled objects in the movie *Avatar* into reality. Simultaneously, the US Department of Defense secretly develops a "mind-reading helmet" capable of reading soldiers' brainwaves. Wearing this helmet, soldiers can read each other's brain activities without speaking.

It's foreseeable that thought-controlled weapons based on BCI technology will equip troops, leading to a new mode of future warfare. Imagine the future battlefield, where human soldiers will only serve as neural system controllers of the "cloud brain," staying away from the bloody battlefield. They interact with the "cloud brain" using their intellect, remotely controlling unmanned drones, armored vehicles, and super-machine warriors at the frontline.

Another application of brain-nets in warfare is "mind control," which is even more powerful than brain-controlled weapons. The core concept of "mind control" involves collecting the enemy soldiers' brainwaves, deciphering their brainwave codes, and then generating simulated brainwaves using brainwave coding technology to transmit them to the enemy's brain. Since it's difficult for enemy soldiers to distinguish between real and fake brainwaves, this technology could cause various effects, including interference with the soldiers' thoughts and actions. With "mind control" technology, soldiers could remotely manipulate the thoughts and actions of enemy soldiers on the battlefield. This manipulation could cover various behaviors, from making the enemy lay down their weapons and surrender to causing them to perform specific tasks or actions.

7.2.8 The Rise of Super-Intelligent Organizations

Beyond causing upheavals and revolutions in various societal aspects, brain-nets possess the greater potential to accelerate a "nuclear fission"-like phenomenon in human technological civilization. This could lead to earth-shattering changes in a concise period beyond the accurate prediction of existing mental models.

Brain Nets significantly enhance the information communication rate, leading to the emergence of super-intelligent organizations. These organizations could consist of dozens, hundreds, or even thousands of people and machines working in high-efficiency collaboration.

On one hand, brain-nets will accelerate the sharing of knowledge and information. Traditional knowledge transfer methods depend on books, Internet searches, or educational institutions. However, the advent of brain-nets enables direct transmission of knowledge into the brain, meaning knowledge can be shared instantaneously without the need for translation through text, language, or other mediums.

On the other hand, brain-nets will push scientific research and innovation to new heights. Scientists and researchers can directly share their discoveries, results, and insights, allowing the entire scientific community to rapidly access the latest scientific knowledge. This will aid in accelerating the progress of scientific research, potentially leading to discoveries and solutions. From new drug development in the medical field to innovative solutions in environmental science, brain-nets will provide scientists with more opportunities to collaborate and address global challenges.

Thus, the information intake, cross-verification, integration, and efficiency of collaborative division of labor in these super-intelligent organizations based on brain-nets will continuously reach unprecedented heights. To an external observer, it appears as an indivisible super-intelligent entity with its own consciousness. This is akin to the evolution in biological history, where prokaryotic cells evolved into eukaryotic cells, single cells into multicellular organisms, and monkeys into human societies capable of language and textual cooperation. This potential is boundless and unstoppable.

As Nicolelis proposed, brains will connect through a "Mirror Neuron System," enabling them to share information and coordinate behaviors, forming a Brain Net among individual brains, further processing abstract information from the objective universe within the human species. Under the influence of evolutionary and genetic mechanisms, this network of brains becomes the most powerful intelligent entity in the universe.

Nicolelis believes the brain's intricate neurophysiological characteristics enable the highest level of external information processing—mental abstraction. Supported by evolutionary and genetic mechanisms, the Brain-Net formed by individual human brains becomes the most powerful intelligent entity in the universe, further enhancing humanity's capacity for mental abstraction. The universe provides external information to the human brain, and the human brain constructs abstract representations of this information. We can view this construction process as a continual reduction in dimensions. This process of mental abstraction is further propagated and deepened through the Brain-Net among different individual brains, forming a shared human mental abstraction, thus advancing humanity's understanding and transformation of the universe.

This also shows us that BCIs are not merely a specific technology connecting the brain and computers; they are also a field of study about the relationship between the brain and the universe and between the brain and computers. The answer is clear and strong: the human brain is the center of the universe. The human brain and its Brain-Net, possessing wisdom unattainable by computers, are central. As we avidly discuss AI and BCI technology, we should also engage in profound philosophical and cultural contemplation.

CHAPTER 8

TOWARD THE ERA OF BRAIN-COMPUTER INTERFACES

8.1 The Ethical Challenges of the BCI Era

In an era marked by a technological explosion—room-temperature supercon-ductors, cancer vaccines, customized medications, mechanical reproduction, space colonization, AI, humanoid robots, quantum technology—any break-through in these frontier technologies would profoundly impact human society and raise ethical issues. Among these, the technology with the most substantial and fundamental impact on human societal ethics is the BCI.

Despite witnessing the potential of BCIs, particularly in disease treatment and enhancement of human physiological functions, such as clinical applications in treating depression or ongoing human experiments where paralyzed patients regain motor functions under BCI intervention, we cannot deny that this technology, which acts directly on the human brain and even reads and writes human consciousness, presents significant challenges to human society.

Conflicts in human society, from international disputes to individual conflicts, essentially stem from conflicts of consciousness. When technology can rewrite and read human consciousness and enable consciousness and cognition replacement, societal consciousness and conflicts will no longer depend on the value systems conveyed by education but on those who control this technology.

The potential impacts of BCI technology on human brain usage are also challenging and unpredictable. The human brain is an extremely complex control system, and our current understanding of it, or brain science, still needs to be improved. Interventions in the brain using electronic information and computer technology may lead to negative consequences in consciousness or ultimately cause the brain to lose its original biological thinking function, becoming solely dependent on information provided by BCIs. These issues demand our attention, concern, and contemplation.

The ethical issues triggered by BCIs extend beyond these, including concerns about privacy and informed consent during use, personal identity and autonomy, human enhancement, and technological and social biases. People from different countries, religions, races, and socioeconomic backgrounds have various needs and visions for BCI technology. Therefore, alongside the development of this technology, governments must establish professional review panels to discuss and formulate relevant laws and regulations actively, ensuring that the technology better aids humanity.

While BCIs have broad application prospects in medicine, life sciences, and HCI, showing us a bright future, the ethical issues they bring deserve deep reflection. These issues primarily encompass the following seven aspects:

8.1.1 Privacy Issues

BCI technology can access personal thoughts, consciousness, and emotions, potentially infringing on individual privacy. For instance, hackers might invade BCI systems to steal or pry into personal private thoughts. As BCIs directly connect the human brain with external devices, system breaches could lead to the leakage and misuse of personal privacy. Unauthorized individuals could access and utilize information such as a user's thoughts, emotions, and personality traits. Moreover, hacker attacks may lead to illegal access to user BCI systems, thus obtaining sensitive information and controlling users' thoughts and behaviors.

Furthermore, once BCIs can directly access the Internet, ensuring the authenticity and accuracy of the information obtained becomes a concern. Whether users are using BCI devices or interacting with AI and the Internet, including in a brain network scenario, how personal privacy rights are safeguarded is crucial. The core issue is that these data are the most private, encompassing brain consciousness, the last bastion of human privacy. Any violation of this domain poses a significant threat and challenge to human rights.

8.1.2 Security Issues

BCI technology can read thought signals from brain activity, accessing users' thought processes, including intentions, emotions, and private thoughts. When this thought privacy becomes datafied and readable, a lack of robust protective measures could lead to privacy breaches. Thus, data protection becomes a pressing challenge as BCI technology must process and store large volumes of brainwave data, including sensitive personal identity and health information. Insufficient data protection could lead to privacy breaches and misuse. Unlike general data privacy breaches, the information processed by BCIs is the most crucial data on brain consciousness. Ensuring the security of BCI devices is a new safety issue. These devices must interact with external devices or the Internet for data exchange. If their security is compromised, hacking could lead to remote control over an individual's physical body and thoughts, severely infringing on personal privacy.

The security of information transmission also poses challenges. Data transmission in BCI technology is susceptible to hacking, potentially allowing hackers to steal brainwave data and personal private information, such as passwords and login details. Any security breach could lead to the misuse of BCI technology, remotely controlling an individual's thoughts and actions. Such read-write control could infringe on personal free will and privacy, forcing individuals into actions against their will.

8.1.3 Consciousness Issues

BCI technology could impact human autonomy and human nature. When we can change our thoughts, emotions, or behaviors through a BCI, especially when we can construct brain cognition and read-write brain consciousness, our autonomous consciousness and individual independence may be challenged. This challenge is greater than traditional education, where we have the full right to refuse certain knowledge. Under the application of BCI technology, will organizations controlling this technology interfere with our cognition without our knowledge or consent, even during our sleep? And when our information and knowledge are constructed through BCI technology, is the ontology cognition of humans the brain of the human entity, or just a digital brain? These issues will raise moral questions, including whether using BCIs to enhance individual abilities is permissible or whether such technology should be restricted.

8.1.4 Social Interaction Clearly

BCI technology will have a more profound impact than smartphones and virtual reality devices, as it does not rely on traditional external hardware for interaction but instead constructs and realizes social interaction directly within brain consciousness. This means using BCIs might reduce opportunities for social interaction, as people can interact directly with computers or virtual worlds through the interface, bypassing conventional communication methods. Even language communication and interaction through external devices could be replaced by direct brain consciousness, which could negatively impact social relationships and lead to issues like social isolation and communication barriers.

8.1.5 Moral Responsibility

The introduction of BCI technology may bring moral responsibility issues. For instance, moral controversies may arise when using BCIs for mental tasks such as decision-making, criminal investigation, or military attacks. Unauthorized thought monitoring might involve privacy infringement, especially in using brain monitoring for crime prevention, potentially leading to premature judgments of criminal intentions in the brain. Moreover, the responsibility for criminal acts committed after brain consciousness has been rewritten or replaced without a user's knowledge becomes a complex issue. Enhancing human intelligence and abilities through BCI technology could lead to social inequality and ethical issues, challenging existing legal systems.

8.1.6 Equity Issues

As with current societal technologies, inequality is prevalent, especially in information and healthcare. Only some information is shared equally, and only some medical resources. These disparities are often tied to societal constructs of power and wealth. BCI technology would similarly exhibit differentiated advancements, particularly evident when it allows for digital therapy and access to high-quality information, exacerbating inequality and societal stratification. This technology could lead to societal and national disparities, especially in countries without advanced BCI technology, potentially depriving some people of its benefits.

8.1.7 Governance Issues

Ethical concerns arise regardless of the stage or scenario in which BCI technology is used, including its current primary application in healthcare. For example, when used for medical treatment, BCIs that can control pain perception or emotional states raise ethical questions about individual consciousness and rights, requiring legal constraints. Considering long-term safety and potential side effects, including possible electronic addiction, is crucial when using BCIs for treatment. The development of BCIs has far outpaced existing ethical norms and legal frameworks. Ethical standards and legal regulations for such emerging technology are necessary to protect individual rights and public interests.

BCI technology is undoubtedly epoch-making, with no historical reference and an uncertain future filled with challenges. This technology digitalizes human brain consciousness, bringing transformative impacts exceeding any previous technology. Its widespread application will inevitably raise ethical and technological issues, including privacy, security, autonomy, social equity, etc. Future developments require broader societal involvement in discussions, considering legal, ethical, and social norms to ensure the sustainable development of BCI technology and the balance of human welfare.

8.2 A Myth about "Human" in the Age of Brain-Computer Interfaces

Compared to the current hype around AI and humanoid robots, BCIs may not yet have garnered as much public attention. However, this technology is steadily making its way toward us. From its commercialization in medical applications to the boundless potential demonstrated in education, entertainment, and military fields to future concepts like memory transplantation and brain networks, an era dominated by BCI technology is approaching—a technological age more disruptive and beyond imagination than the era of AI.

8.2.1 The Fusion of Human and Machine Has Begun

The most significant feature of BCI technology is its ability to connect humans and machines. In a sense, the process of human-machine fusion has already begun.

Tens of thousands of people globally have undergone cochlear implant surgery, one of the earliest applications of BCIs. How we perceive sound essentially involves the vibration of air molecules around our heads at specific frequencies. Whether it's the sound of a guitar, a voice, the wind, or anything else, it's produced by vibrations, which cause the surrounding air molecules to vibrate in a similar pattern, spreading outwards like ripples on water. Our ears are machines that convert these air vibrations into electrical pulses. When sound enters our ears through the air, it accurately transforms the medium's vibration pattern into electrical signals, which are then sent to connected nerve endings. This triggers a specific combination of action potentials in the nerves, and the auditory cortex then processes the signal. This process of receiving sound information is what we call "hearing."

Cochlear implants work on a similar principle. They receive external sounds and convert them into electrical signals, directly transmitting them to the auditory nerves in the brain. In essence, a cochlear implant is an artificial ear capable of replicating the process of the sound-pulse-auditory nerve that a normal ear performs. It replaces the human "ear," if desired; its capabilities can surpass those of a normal ear, allowing one to hear sounds previously imperceptible to human ears.

Similar revolutionary advancements are occurring in vision restoration, like retinal prosthetics. Blindness is usually a result of retinal degeneration. In such cases, retinal prosthetics can restore vision similarly to cochlear implants (though not as directly). They replicate the functions of a normal eye, transmitting information as electronic pulses to the nerves.

Retinal prosthetics represent a more complex form of BCI than cochlear implants. In 2011, the first FDA-approved retinal prosthetic, "Argus II," produced by Second Sight, was released. It has 60 sensors, whereas a real retina has about one million neurons. Although it's still rudimentary, allowing for the perception of vague edges, shapes, and light-dark variations, it significantly improves complete blindness. However, we don't necessarily need one million sensors to achieve substantial vision—simulations show that retinal prosthetics with 600 to 1,000 electrodes could provide enough vision for reading and facial recognition.

Similarly, mechanical prosthetics and even brain chips are following this path, though they are currently used for medical purposes to treat or restore bodily functions. However, it's foreseeable that one day, they will also be applied to healthy individuals, aiming to "enhance" rather than "restore" bodily functions.

Today, enhancing everyday sensory and cognitive abilities through brain chips is becoming feasible. With artificial cochlear implants (which may be called something else by then), all functions will be integrated into a small hardware device implantable in the brain, allowing us to hear high-frequency sounds previously unheard by humans. Perhaps you could set the frequency to a dog's hearing range and experience the world as they do. Or, through retinal prosthetics, we might see specific types of light emitted by objects in the dark, which are normally invisible to the human eye. It could even allow us to see ultraviolet light.

In such a future world, BCIs will provide us with entirely new experiences, enriching our perceptions in unprecedented ways.

8.2.2 Breaking Biological Boundaries of the Brain

The most thrilling prospect of human-machine fusion lies in integrating BCIs and AI.

Indeed, from the inception of humanity, human evolution has been accelerating. This process spanned billions of years, from the emergence of the earliest life forms on earth to the Cambrian explosion. The transition from the Cambrian explosion to multicellular organisms took hundreds of millions of years; from fish to mammals, millions of years; from mammals to Homo sapiens, hundreds of thousands of years; and from Homo sapiens to modern humans, tens of thousands of years. In the transition from Homo sapiens to modern humans, with the rapid development of technology, humans have been using technology to expand control over nature, thereby dominating more limited resources, ensuring safety, stabilizing food supply, and creating superior environments, further propelling evolution.

Now, biological transformation projects like BCIs are accelerating the pace of the evolution of human life. Looking ahead, when human intelligence is linked with AI, humanity will completely break through the limits of individual intelligence. This breaks the norm of gradually learning from childhood through college and even, to some extent, allows direct reading of electronic documents by the brain instead of through the eyes. Moreover, everyone's brain might be connected to computers and other people's brains. Human intelligence will be interconnected in some form, furthering the development of AI. Then, human brains, or thoughts, will control everything, from self-driving cars to smart homes. Everything in human activity will start and end with the brain. Simultaneously, humans will evolve into a new species, ushering civilization into a new phase.

Professor Nicolelis has also envisaged the ultimate future of human-machine fusion in interviews—the interaction between the brain and AI could be an adventure, with our brains being reshaped. They will gradually adapt to grasping virtual objects, operating computers, and communicating through thoughts, especially with other interesting brains in our favorite "brain networks"—the ultimate version of social networks.

The "exoskeleton" at the 2014 World Cup opening ceremony, which amazed the world, will seem like a primitive, rough, and clumsy child's toy. Future "exoskeleton" systems might resemble Iron Man's "mechanical battle suit," giving ordinary people superhuman strength, sensations, and abilities. Humans will appear in various remote environments by controlling robotic avatars, bio-humans, or clones through thoughts. Things that sound unimaginable today will become commonplace in the future. From the depths of the ocean to the forbidden zones of supernovae and even the tiny crevices in the cells of our bodies, the human reach will eventually match our insatiable ambition for exploration.

Our brains will complete their epic journey of liberation, breaking free from bodies that have inhabited the earth for millions of years, using bidirectional

BCIs to operate myriad tools. They will become our new eyes, ears, and hands in the micro-world created by nature. The world is composed of atoms or cells, and while our bodies can never enter the realm of atoms or cells, our thoughts can effortlessly and unhesitatingly penetrate them.

We might remotely operate various shapes and sizes of robots and spaceships to explore other planets at the edge of the universe on our behalf, storing strange terrains and landscapes within reach of our mental tentacles. With each step in exploration, tools created by future generations will continue to be assimilated by their brains, further expanding their selves and defining their perspectives. All this will far exceed our current imagination.

8.2.3 Opening the Door to the Future of Humanity

With the continuous advancement and innovation of BCI technology, the future of downloading knowledge, transplanting memories, telepathic communication, and brain networking will no longer be mere figments of science fiction but real-life experiences.

The need for years to master a skill or acquire professional knowledge will be obsolete. Just as one downloads a song or a movie online, knowledge and skills can be downloaded. Learning and education will become unprecedentedly convenient. Everything can be accomplished instantly, whether it's learning a new language, mastering a craft, or understanding the latest scientific discoveries. Knowledge will no longer be confined to books or classrooms; it will be an omnipresent resource accessible through mere thought, enabling you to acquire new skills or explore new areas.

Furthermore, we can record, upload, and share our memories. Gone will be the pain of forgetfulness and the loss of precious moments to time. Our most cherished memories can be preserved, shared with loved ones, or even passed down to future generations, deepening our connections with each other.

Further advancement in BCI technology will make interpersonal communication more profound and interesting. Telepathic communication will no longer be fiction but reality. Friends, family, and even strangers will be able to convey information through thought, eliminating barriers to language and culture. This will lead to greater collaboration and understanding, making it easier to form deep emotional bonds.

The concept of a "brain network" will also become a reality. People will be able to communicate and collaborate on a mental level through interconnected brain interfaces. This will drive the progress of human society, accelerating scientific research and technological innovation and providing new approaches to solving global issues. We will enter a new era of interconnected thinking, paving a novel path for the evolution of human civilization.

Just as the Human Genome Project changed the landscape of science and medicine, the breakthroughs in BCI technology will not only provide us with unparalleled insight into the brain but also create new industrial sectors, stimulate economic activities, and fundamentally reshape our way of life, causing major shifts in politics, economy, society, and culture.

This also raises the ultimate philosophical question: Who am I? When consciousness can be uploaded to a computer, will humans achieve digital immortality? When our physical bodies perish, can our souls exist eternally? When we finally conquer death—the origin of all human desires and fears—are we still human, or have we become gods? Have we completed the ultimate evolution of humanity, or are we heading toward the extinction of our species?

From a practical perspective or considering specific scenarios, BCIs undoubtedly present a utilitarian hope and tremendous social value. Yet, they also carry an ultimate myth about "humanity" concerning the boundaries of technological needs and the limits of technological logic.

Underneath the enthusiasm for technology lies its ultimate essence: How to use an increasingly embodied technology to achieve connection and interaction between humans and machines without implanting machinery into the flesh. This involves a deeper issue: how much control do our bodies and brains want? Or what preparations have we made to relinquish control?

Regardless, a glorious, destiny-reshaping, brand-new scientific vista is unfolding before us. We are entering a new era of BCIs.

REFERENCES

Artery Orange. *Global Medical + Brain-Computer Interface Value Trends Report 2022 Q1.* 2022.

Chen, Jingjing, Wang Fei, Gao Xiaorong, et al. "Applications of Brain-Machine Interfaces in the Education Field: Trends and Challenges." *Science and Technology Review* 40, no. 12 (2022): 90–101.

Chen, Qi, Yuan Tianwei, Zhang Liwen, et al. "Current Research and Trends in the Development of Brain-Computer Interface Medical Applications." *Journal of Biomedical Engineering* 40, no.03 (2023): 566–572.

Chen, Yan. *A Brief History of Brain-Computer Interfaces.*

China Academy of Information and Communications Technology. *Brain-Computer Interface Overall Vision and Key Technology Research Report.*

China Artificial Intelligence Industry Development Alliance. *White Paper on the Application of Brain-Computer Interface Technology in the Medical and Health Field.* 2021.

Danke Research Institute. *2022 Brain-Computer Interface Industry Research Report: Focus on Enhancement, Scene Implementation, and Technological Iteration.* 2022.

Drew, Liam. "Decoding the Business of Brain–Computer Interfaces." *Nature Electronics*, 2023.

Ferry, Luc. *The Transhuman Revolution.*

REFERENCES

Ge, Song, Xu Jingjing, Lai Shunnan, et al. "Brain-Computer Interfaces: Current Status, Issues, and Prospects." *Progress in Biochemistry and Biophysics* 47, no. 12 (2020): 1227–1249. doi:10.16476/j.pibb.2020.0072.

Guosen Securities. *Special Research on the Metaverse Industry: Current Status and Future of Brain-Computer Interfaces.*

Guotai Junan Securities. *Brain-Machine Technology Special Research Report: A New Path for Human-Machine Interaction.*

Ji, Bowen, and Yin Erwei. "Military Applications Status and Future of Brain-Computer Interface Technology."

Jiang, Linxing, Stocco Andrea, Losey Darby M, Abernethy Justin A, Prat Chantel S, and Rao Rajesh P N. "BrainNet: A Multi-person Brain-to-Brain Interface for Direct Collaboration between Brains." *Scientific Reports* (2019).

Jiang, Liyong, Liu Shu, Diao Tianxi, et al. "Advancements in Brain-Computer Interface Technology and Potential Military Medical Applications." *Military Medicine* 45, no. 10 (2021): 780–785.

Kagaku, Michihiro. *The Future of the Mind.*

Li, Dan, Liu Lingyu, Jin Lingjing, et al. "Research Progress on Rehabilitation Training Based on Brain-Computer Interface in Upper Limb Rehabilitation After Stroke." *Chinese Rehabilitation* 38, no. 10 (2023): 621–625.

Liang, Wendong, Guo Xiaohui, Cheng Bo, et al. "Advances in the Application of Brain-Computer Interfaces in Rehabilitation Medicine." *Medical Equipment* 35, no. 21 (2022): 193–196.

Liu, Xinyu, Wang Dongyun, and Shi Li. "Brain-Computer Interface Education Applications: Principles, Potential, and Challenges." *Open Education Research* 29, no. 01 (2023): 18–25. doi:10.13966/j.cnki.kfjyyj.

Luo, Jianggong, Ding Peng, Gong Anmin, et al. "Applications, Industrial Transformation, and Commercial Value of Brain-Computer Interface Technology." *Journal of Biomedical Engineering* 39, no. 02 (2022): 405–415.

Mitchell, Peter, Lee Sarah C M Yoo, Peter E, Morokoff Andrew, Sharma Rahul P, Williams Daryl L, MacIsaac Christopher, et al. "Assessment of Safety of a Fully Implanted Endovascular Brain-Computer Interface for Severe Paralysis in 4 Patients: The Stentrode with Thought-Controlled Digital Switch (SWITCH) Study." *JAMA Neurology* (2023).

REFERENCES

Nicolelis, Miguel. *Brain-Machine Transcendence: How Brain-Computer Interfaces Are Changing the Future of Humanity.*

Nijholt, Anton, Contreras Vidal, Jose Luis, Jeunet Camille, and Väljamäe, Aleksander. "Editorial: Brain-Computer Interfaces for Non-clinical (Home, Sports, Art, Entertainment, Education, Well-Being) Applications." *Frontiers in Computer Science* (2022).

Rao, Rajesh P.N. *Introduction to Brain-Computer Interfaces.*

Reinhart, Robert M G, and Nguyen John A. "Working Memory Revived in Older Adults by Synchronizing Rhythmic Brain Circuits." *Nature Neuroscience* (2019).

Valeriani, Davide, Cecotti Hubert, Thelen Antonia, and Herff Christian. "Editorial: Translational Brain-Computer Interfaces: From Research Labs to the Market and Back." *Frontiers in Human Neuroscience* (2023).

Yi, Qi. "In Conversation with BrainCo Strong Brain Technology: Science Fiction World of Bionic Limbs Becoming Reality."

Yuan, Mingyang. "Ethical Reflections on Brain-Computer Interfaces for Human Extension in the Era of the Intelligent Revolution." *Medicine and Philosophy* 43, no. 03 (2022): 17–21.

Zhang, Ling, and Gao Xiaorong. "Fifty Years of Brain-Computer Interfaces."

Zhang, Tiankan. "Brain-Computer Interfaces Are Finally Here! Will They Open Pandora's Box?"

Zhongguancun Industry Research Institute, and Fan Hao. *Seven Globally Notable Brain-Computer Interface Representative Companies (Part 1).*

Zhongshang Industry. "Research and Analysis of the 2023 Chinese Brain-Computer Interface Industry Chain Map."

Zhu, Yashu, and Hu Xing. *2023 Brain-Computer Interface Industry Atlas.* 2023.

INDEX

ABOUT THE AUTHOR

Kevin Chen is a renowned science and technology writer and scholar. He was a visiting scholar at Columbia University, a postdoctoral scholar at the University of Cambridge, and an invited course professor at Peking University. He has served as a special commentator and columnist for the *People's Daily*, CCTV, China Business Network, SINA, NetEase, and many other media outlets. He has published monographs in numerous domains, including finance, science and technology, real estate, medical treatments, and industrial design. He currently lives in Hong Kong.